FRANZ
FERDINAND

AND THE
POP RENAISSANCE

FRANZ FERDINAND

AND THE
POP RENAISSANCE

HAMILTON HARVEY

REYNOLDS & HEARN LTD
LONDON

PICTURE CREDITS
JACKET
FRONT AND BACK: Brian Rasic/Rex Features
SPINE: Charles Sykes/Rex Features

PICTURE SECTION 1
PAGE 1: Sipa Press/Rex Features
PAGES 2 & 3: Hamilton Harvey
PAGES 4 & 5: André Csillag/Rex Features
PAGE 6A & B: Brian Rasic/Rex Features
PAGE 7A-D: Hamilton Harvey; 7E: André Csillag/Rex Features
PAGE 8: Brian Rasic/Rex Features

PICTURE SECTION 2
PAGE 1: Matt Sadler/Rex Features
PAGE 2: Geoff Robinson/Rex Features
PAGE 3: Geoff Robinson/Rex Features
PAGES 4 & 5: Richard Young/Rex Features
PAGE 6A: Geoff Robinson/Rex Features; 6B: Brian Rasic/Rex Features
PAGE 8: Charles Sykes/Rex Features

First published in 2005 by
Reynolds & Hearn Ltd
61a Priory Road
Kew Gardens
Richmond
Surrey TW9 3DH

© Hamilton Harvey 2005

A CIP catalogue record for this book is available from the British Library.
ISBN 1 905287 00 3

Designed by Peri Godbold.

Printed and bound in Great Britain by Biddles Ltd, King's Lynn, Norfolk.

CONTENTS

ACKNOWLEDGEMENTS

The author would like to thank the following for their
help with this book:

Amanda Mackinnon, Sorcha Dallas, Sarah Lowndes,
Hannah Robinson, Robert Johnston, Martin Cloonan, Keith McIvor,
Natasha Noramly, Malcolm Jack, Colin Hardie, Jim McCulloch,
Ian Sinclair, John Robertson, Andy Kemp, Stephen Fall,
Marcus Hearn, Richard Reynolds, Peri Godbold, Jill Mingo,
Andy Miller and Brendan O'Hare. And C.

1.

WELL, THAT WAS EASY

At the end of 2004, four tired musicians returned to Glasgow. They had set out from the city as a popular local act, but were returning as global stars with a multi-million- selling album and a slew of hit singles. From being unknowns just over a year before, their faces were now well known from the UK to the USA, from mainland Europe to Australia and Japan. For Franz Ferdinand, 2004 had been the make-or-break year, and they had thrown their all into making it. The effort had demanded a high price of them: mental and physical exhaustion had almost led to the band breaking up after a dispute in Paris in November. Now, however, they had made it back to dry land, and had time to think about the next step on the path – their second album.

Ahead of them lay five months in a farmhouse in the rolling Lanarkshire countryside, half an hour from Glasgow. Alex Kapranos had bought the house – with its acres of land and plenty of outhouses – as the new Franz headquarters before Christmas. It was the first time the band had owned its own property and not lived under constant threat of eviction. This retreat to rugged rural bliss followed a year and a half during which they were rarely in the same place two nights in a row. There could have been a risk that the sudden seclusion and permanence of the Kapranos farm would rob the band of the energy that had propelled them to their phenomenal success – and, in some respects, this seemed to have proved the case – but only in a positive sense. The time and space was essential not only to work on the second album, but also allow Franz to get grounded once again.

In fact, as 2004 came to an end, the band envisaged that the new album would be out by the spring or early summer. It was not an unreasonable assumption, as Alex and Nick McCarthy had been composing on the road and had already written enough to make up an album. Also, a band as used to connecting with their fans on a regular basis as Franz Ferdinand might naturally have worried that a long time away would risk their public image fading. To prevent fans losing touch with the band, Franz made full use of the Internet. Through their official website (franzferdinand.co.uk), not to be confused with the equally impressive fan-run sites (franzferdinand.org and franzferdinand.net), the band were able to post regular diary entries, both text and video, as well as a series of digital snaps showing life at the farm. Almost every day, fans were able to peer through the keyhole, in a sort of Franz Ferdinand version of *Big Brother*. We were able to peer in nosily as the band, often unshaven and bleary-eyed, fiddled about in the studio being built at the farm. We observed Alex chopping wood for the fire in the cold winter months, inspected a pot of soup being prepared for lunch, and caught a glimpse of Nick staring dreamily into space one morning, thinking about... who knows.

The regular web appearances gave thousands of fans around the world the chance to look in on the band – in a very intimate way. It was a way for the band to seem within reach, but in fact to remain in the privacy of the farm. As Chris Hassell – new media director at DS.Emotion – the company that set up the website – proudly stated: 'The interactive, personal, engaging, live and constantly updated footage helps to build strong, personal relationships with a hard-to-reach, young net-savvy audience.' In other words, the day-to-day pictures and mini-adventures captured on digital photograph and video helped to create the sense that we were actually part of Franz Ferdinand's gaggle of friends and colleagues. Except, of course, there was nothing personal about it, especially when DS.Emotion reported that there were 15,000 new visitors to the site every day, and 450,000 every month. That's more 'strong, personal relationships' than Franz could have hoped to establish in many months of touring.

The farm allowed the band to get on with the writing and initial recording of the second album away from the chaos of the road, and also offered a quiet atmosphere where they could avoid feeling pressured by the expectations surrounding the follow-up to their hugely successful and critically acclaimed debut. Second albums are always crucial to a band's continuing success, but somehow Franz's follow-up seemed more critical than usual. Another of the key benefits that the time awarded Franz for the composition of the album was the chance to thoroughly edit first drafts of songs into polished, finished works. This was a process that the band went through during the creation of the first album, and Alex values it as the only way to produce good pop songs. He told the *NME* in April 2005: 'What's difficult to do on the road is get some perspective and do the thing which makes songs good, which is editing them down and discarding the bits that are rubbish. We do that from the four of us just sitting around and chatting about it, seeing what we like and what we don't like.'

Another benefit of taking time over the second album was that the band had a chance to move on musically. Alex told the *Scotland on Sunday*[1] paper that he wanted to avoid falling into the trap of sounding the same: 'If you slip into predictability, it is the death of your band.' Moving on also allowed the band to shift itself to suit the global audience its first album had managed to reach – especially the thousands of punters who forked out for the album in the States. To further connect with this substantial US audience, Alex delved into American culture for inspiration in his song writing.

Alex's entries in the diary section of the band's website disclosed some of the influences that he was drawing on in his lyric writing. He reported that he had been reading the poems of Charles Bukowski, especially the collection *Play the Piano Drunk Like a Percussion Instrument Until the Fingers Begin to Bleed a Bit*. Bukowski (1920–1994) is one of the biggest-selling poets in America, occupying more bookshelf space than any other US poet. Despite this mass appeal (by the standards of poetry, anyway), he retains a reputation as an underground poet. This is largely due to the nature of his writing, which, with its brutal, sordid honesty and stubborn avoidance of finesse, continues successfully to avoid official acceptance into the literary canon. Some professors of literature have even denied that it is worthy of printing at all. In his more than sixty books of poems, short stories and novels, Bukowski's main source was always his own life – basically that of an alcohol-fuelled sex addict living in Los Angeles. At first glance, the Beat rantings of a pockmarked alcoholic might not seem the best source of inspiration for Alex in writing song lyrics, but there are some important points of contact. The balance that Bukowski maintained between underground (or indie in music terms) and mainstream is also one of

1. 29 May 2005.

the many tightropes that Franz Ferdinand have so far trodden with admirable skill. Also, Bukowski's poems, while containing heavyweight themes, are usually easily accessible, one of the reasons he continues from beyond the grave to foster a cult following among students.

Another cult hero from the New World mentioned by Alex as an inspiration during the creation of the second album was Bob Dylan. Having listened to a lot of Dylan during the writing and recording of the album, he tried to bring something of the great American songwriter's approach into his own work. Colin Somerville, music critic for *Scotland on Sunday*[2], suspected the Dylan factor might have been part of a deliberate attempt to develop a sound more friendly to American ears: 'Their first album was very well received, but Kapranos has been at it long enough to know that you have to move on pretty sharply and perhaps consolidate their position in America with a more folksy sound.' Joe Mott of the *Daily Star* managed to stretch the Dylan factor even further. He claimed in his 'Joe Mott's Hot' page that it was the soothing influence of the American bard that was responsible for Franz Ferdinand's restored relations after their occasional flare-ups on the road in 2004: 'Scots Rockers Cut Out the In-Fighting... Thanks to Dylan.'

As well as Dylan, Franz have also been listening to contemporary R&B, including artists such as Lil' Jon and Kanye West, in an attempt to keep up with what's happening at the cutting-edge of pop music in the States. While they can't hope and probably wouldn't want to be directly musically or lyrically influenced by R&B, Alex explained to the *NME*'s Barry Nicolson in July that 'when you listen to the sound of those records, the energy, the preciseness, the inventiveness... that's inspiring.' Another important American influence on the second album was its producer, Rich Costey. He was to many an intriguing and unexpected choice, but, in the light of the band's desire to move on and out to broader musical horizons, a choice that makes a lot of sense. Costey's work on Muse's 2003 album *Absolution* helped that band to establish a strong foothold in the States, having already built a loyal fan base in the UK. It was obviously hoped that his input would do the same for Franz Ferdinand, who had already made considerable inroads into the American market with their first album.

2. Ibid.

However, Costey was not just seen as a ticket to mainstream American success, as the list of his past clients showed. He had worked with an excitingly diverse group of artists, from Minimalist composer Philip Glass to bands such as Rage Against the Machine, Bloc Party, Nine Black Alps, New Order, Polyphonic Spree and Doves. His past credits also included production and mixing for Franz Ferdinand's re-recording of 'This Fire' (renamed 'This Fffire') as a single for the US market. The introduction was obviously successful and Costey agreed to spend a few months of early 2005 shacked up with the band in the wilds of the Scottish countryside – an indication of his dedication at the very least. The distance between New York and Glasgow was demonstrated during a night out on the town with the band. Walking down Sauchiehall Street on their way to a gig, the band encountered the critical judgement of a group of revellers. They took particular exception to Costey's choice of a bright-red corduroy jacket, demanding ''Ere, pal, are you a magician?' Costey might have mused that it would have taken more than a bright-red corduroy jacket to turn heads in Manhattan.

Nevertheless, the time spent in Lanarkshire with the band was fruitful, and Franz and he left Glasgow for New York at the end of May with 16 songs recorded, enough to provide a pool from which to select the strongest for the album. Through June and into July, Franz worked with Costey at his main workplace, Avatar Studios, formerly known as Power Station, accepted since its creation in 1977 as one of the best recording spaces in the world. The studio complex, situated on the West Side on 53rd Street between Ninth and Tenth Avenues, was built into the shell of the old Consolidated Edison power station responsible for providing electricity to much of New York. Power Station was established by Tony Bongiovi, one of America great producers, who started out in Motown in the 1960s and worked with many of the most important artists in US musical history, including Jimi Hendrix, Talking Heads and the Ramones. Bongiovi sold Power Station in 1996, whereupon it took on its new identity as Avatar Studios, but with much of the interior and equipment intact. The crowning glory of the complex is the cathedral-like Studio A, a vast wood-clad space with room for a full orchestra of 60 musicians. Avatar Studios' list of previous clients is long and impressive (David Bowie, Roxy Music, Bob Dylan, Bruce Springsteen, Björk, Iggy Pop and Ozzy Osbourne have all recorded there).

The songs that emerged from the Glasgow/New York recording process to make up *You Could Have It So Much Better... With Franz Ferdinand* were the final proof that the band did indeed manage to move on without losing their identity in the process. The first surprise for fans was that the album would have a title, early reports having indicated that it would simply be called *Franz Ferdinand*. The strong design of the first album, with its Constructivist/Dadaist echoes, was retained, but with a different colour scheme: this time a striking red, black and green combination. There was also a surprise for the pundits expecting that the Bob Dylan influence referred to by Alex might have resulted in a folkier sound. While Alex did bring lessons learnt from Dylan's work into his lyrics – which were markedly darker and more intense than those of the debut – the sound of the album was still driven by Nick. The result was an album that expressed a growing musical confidence and a willingness to explore areas of music other than the guitar pop of *Franz Ferdinand*. The opening passage of the 'The Fallen,'[3] for example, is far heavier in tone and sheer raucousness than anything from the first album and takes the band into rock, rather than pop, territory. While the album pushed the decibel levels with 'The Fallen', it also contained quieter moments such as 'Walk Away', an acoustic song first performed shortly after its composition on tour in Japan in November.[4]

There were also more familiar sounds, such as the first single from the album, 'Do You Want To', released in September, with the regular repetition of its catchy chorus giving it a similar structure to 'Take Me Out'. 'Outsiders' also fits the original manifesto of guitar music that girls can dance to, mixing a driving baseline with Nick's powerful chord progression. The album's title track originated in a set of 'Smells Like Teen Spirit'-esque chords that Nick concocted one day at the farm. Alex was so excited by Nick's creation that he rushed off to write the lyrics before the moment was lost; the band then immediately ran through the song to ensure they had truly captured it. Other songs, like 'This

---

3. The song was first performed at the Albert Hall in April 2005 with the title 'Robert Anderson Is Christ'. Written about a Glasgow friend of the band, it was decided to remove his name from the song in respect of his privacy. Unfortunately, the playlist for the Albert Hall show was photographed and titles passed on to the media.

4. The debut performance was part of the acoustic set the band played while Bob Hardy was in hospital with gastroenteritis.

Boy' and 'I'm Your Villain', had been around for a long time and had gone through a long process of evolution.

In short, *You Could Have It So Much Better... With Franz Ferdinand* showed the band expanding and moving out from the first album. Not afraid to explore new territory, but also unwilling to bow to pressure to create something utterly different from their previous work in order to avoid cries of 'it's all the same', Franz Ferdinand demonstrated that they were capable of maturing naturally and with integrity.

2.
AN ELEGANT TOWN

G lasgow's fortune as a city was linked for much if its existence with the rise of the New World. The city took over from Aberdeen and Leith (on the east coast and so serving European destinations) as the principal port of Scotland while trade links with the colonies across the Atlantic developed. Glasgow is situated on the River Clyde, which flows out to the west coast and offers ships a route to carry their cargo inland. Before this rise to affluence, Glasgow had been a small but beautiful town growing up around its cathedral (founded in 1136) and university (founded in 1451). The city spread out from the cross formed by the Trongate and Gallowgate running along the Clyde, and High Street and Salt Market Street running to and from the river.

The Act of Union in 1707 (bringing Scotland under the government of England), which many Glaswegians had been bitterly opposed to, ironically brought Glasgow into its first period of prosperity. The Navigation Acts had hindered Scottish merchants from trading with the New World, but after Union, such barriers were lifted and business flourished. Within a few decades, Glasgow had spawned its first generation of 'tobacco lords', who built lavish townhouses in the city and raised the city's outlook and ambition. As well as tobacco, the import of sugar and rum brought wealth to the city. The city grew with the inflow of riches, but managed to retain its charm and proportions. The *Encyclopaedia Britannica* of 1771 described Glasgow as 'one of the most elegant towns in Scotland', a description that would have seemed inappropriate just a few decades later. By the last twenty years of the eighteenth century, the focus of the city's wealth had shifted from New World imports to manufacturing linen and cotton fabric. This shift came with the birth of the Industrial Revolution, and by the second decade of the nineteenth century Glasgow had changed beyond recognition into a city of cotton mills, complete with smoking chimneys from the furnaces powering the steam engines invented by Glasgow's industrial hero James Watt. Glasgow became a centre of engineering excellence and a producer of machinery to drive the Industrial Revolution. Combined with its long association with sea travel, this local mechanical skill soon logically turned itself to steam-ship building. This was the start of the industry that would lead to Glasgow's next great era of prosperity and huge expansion. During the nineteenth century, Glasgow grew from a small provincial city to the Second City of the British Empire. Unfortunately, the population grew so fast that not even the frenetic building habits of the Victorian Glaswegians could meet the demand. It was ironically during this period of its greatest fortune that Glasgow's infamous slums developed.

Religion has always played an important part in Glasgow's character. In the early days this was the positive influence of the cathedral that formed the heart and *raison d'être* of the city. After the Reformation, however, the influence religion played began to sour. The dominant merchant class was mostly Protestant and, therefore, so was the Glasgow Corporation, the city's local government. The bulk of the working immigrants to the city, from the eighteenth century onwards, were Catholic – many coming to escape poverty in Ireland. This fundamental imbalance between a Protestant elite and a Catholic working class set up the split personality that has at times threatened to tear Glasgow apart. The two camps were even given their own football clubs with the foundation of Rangers in 1872 and Celtic in 1888.

3.
ARRESTS AND AWARDS

ranz Ferdinand were not completely trapped at the farm during the five months of recording. They left for New York directly from Russia, following their first performance on Russian soil on 19 and 20 May 2005. The shows took place largely thanks to the band's number one fan in Russia, namely the DJ, TV talk-show host, music journalist and academic, Artemy 'Art' Troitsky, referred to by bass player Bob Hardy as 'John Peelmanov'. Troitsky had long been trumpeting the talents of Franz Ferdinand and invited them to play a series of shows. Seemingly overwhelmed that Franz were indeed coming to play in his back yard, Troitsky heralded their arrival with a typically resounding sound bite: 'This is the third band in the history of rock after the Beatles and Nirvana.' Troitsky is well known for his dramatic statements concerning his favourite bands, perhaps the most famous being his pronouncement that 'The Beatles ... have done more for the fall of Communism than any other western institution.'

Troitsky helped to develop a groundswell of support for Franz, and the shows (in St Petersburg and in Moscow) were sold out a month ahead, and consisted of hordes of fans who knew the song lyrics better than the band. They particularly appreciated the performances of the 'Michael' B-side 'Love and Destroy', with its mention of 'the Muscovites' sky' in each verse. The whole song refers to the 1930s novel *The Master and Margarita* by Russian author Mikhail Bulgakov – one of Alex's favourite books. The novel was written at the height of Stalin's reign of terror over the Soviet Union and uses magic realism to satirise the regime. Anything more direct or obvious would have led to a death sentence. Little did Alex realise when he arrived in Moscow that he was soon to have his own taste of state displeasure.

The band had been due to head on to Estonia, Latvia and Iceland after the Russian shows, but their recording schedule demanded that they cancel or postpone these appearances and head straight for New York. However, at Moscow's Domodedovo Airport, about to board a flight for

New York, things started to go wrong. While the rest of the band and crew were filing through passport control unmolested, Alex was held back by the officials. At first, it seemed that some routine check was being made, but when uniformed soldiers and officers appeared on the scene, it became obvious that the situation was serious. A series of tense interviews followed, and it emerged that the Russian officials considered Alex a 'high-level security risk'. This bizarre allegation meant Alex would have to be arrested, and taken back into the centre of Moscow to the Federal Security Service headquarters for questioning as a spy. Before he was bundled off into some Moscow cellar, however, the truth emerged. Alex's passport still bears the surname Huntley, his mother's maiden name, which he adopted when the family moved to Sunderland. This, it turned out, was the name selected by the British MI6 spy Richard Tomlinson as an alias during a mission to Moscow in 1992. Tomlinson was a high-flying agent who was chosen for an important and extremely clandestine mission to Moscow to recover Russian missile test reports. The reports had been stolen by a colonel in the Russian army and hidden in a sewing box in his mother-in-law's flat on the outskirts of Moscow. Tomlinson arrived in Moscow as Alex Huntley, an Anglo-Argentine businessman who was on his way to attend a three-day *Financial Times* symposium at the Metropol Hotel in Moscow. The disguise worked, and 'Huntley' managed to smuggle the missile reports out of the country in a copy of the *Financial Times*. The name was logged by Russian intelligence once the leak became public knowledge. They must have thought it was their lucky day when 'Huntley' apparently reappeared, this time in the unlikely alias of an indie pop star, complete with band and road crew. Tomlinson went on to gain celebrity when he was sacked from MI6 and retaliated by revealing his secrets in a novel, *The Big Breach*. An ironic twist to the tail is that Tomlinson was originally from New Zealand, the country where the real Alex Huntley had his first run-in with airport security, although that time it was for attempting to smuggle an orange into the country rather than for international espionage.

Other excursions from the farm included an outing in April to play at the Albert Hall in the fifth annual benefit concert for the Teenage Cancer Trust, appearing on the bill with the Magic Numbers, Graham Coxon (ex-Blur guitarist) and Kaiser Chiefs. Before this, in February, Franz did a mini-tour of France for the benefit of NRJ Radio listeners, as well as another benefit appearance at the Scottish Exhibition and Conference Centre in Glasgow to raise money for the Indonesian Tsunami appeal, this time sharing the work with Idlewild, Belle and Sebastian and Texas, among others. February also saw a clutch of award ceremonies to attend – the Shockwave *NME* Awards in Hammersmith, the Grammys in LA and the Brit Awards in Earls Court.

The Brit Awards saw them pitched against Keane, the Hastings trio who had emerged around the same time as Franz and who had made a similar splash, but with very different music. In many ways, Keane represented the other option for pop, the Travis-Coldplay route that is just as comfortable on Radio 2 as on Radio 1. The Brit Awards was the first time that Franz's post-punk, guitar-based approach would be directly judged against Keane's well-crafted, piano-based ballads. Franz Ferdinand were nominated for five categories: British Rock Act, British Group, British Album, British Breakthrough Act and British Live Act, three of which Keane were also nominated for. Franz accepted an invitation to perform at the event, and delivered the ever-impressive 'Take Me Out' to an audience comprised of record-industry types and hordes of ticket-buying fans. As far as the Keane-Franz battle was concerned, Franz came out on top, winning two of their five nominated categories: Best British Rock Act and Best British Group – which they dedicated to John Peel, who had died in October 2004. Keane walked away with Best British Album.

Close on the heels of the Brits came the Grammy Awards, the US record industry's back-slapping session. Franz Ferdinand had garnered an impressive three nominations as well as an invitation to perform at the ceremony, which they duly accepted, again with a performance of 'Take Me Out'. For a new British band to have such a high profile at the Grammys was impressive enough, even though they came away empty-handed, losing out to U2's 'Vertigo' in Best Rock Performance and Best Music Video (Short Form) and to Wilco's *A Ghost Is Born* in Best Alternative Music Album. They were back on top just four days later at the Shockwave *NME* Awards, however, where five nominations converted into two wins for Best Album and Best Track for 'Take Me Out'.

4.
DRINKING MUSIC

hroughout the nineteenth century, Glasgow was a sometimes turbulent mixing pot for a number of different musical traditions. While the predominantly Protestant middle class enjoyed musical soirées, dances and the bawdier entertainment to be found at the drinking clubs that were popular into the early 1800s, the cultural life of the predominantly Catholic working class centred around the pub. Many of Glasgow's public houses held Saturday night 'singsongs' or 'free and easies' – forerunners of modern-day karaoke nights – in which punters were encouraged or cajoled to contribute a song or act from the floor by an overbearing character known as 'the Chairman'. The music performed varied from folk to popular ballads to political chants and even hymns, whatever the unfortunate performer could bring to mind when the Chairman swooped. These sing-alongs provided welcome relief and release for the city's workers, who spent long hours in workshops and cotton mills in exchange for pitifully low wages. However, the middle class frowned upon these sometimes-wild entertainments, and viewed them as a symptom of the proletariat's descent into depravity through the misuse of alcohol.

Drink was indeed a growing problem, with spirit consumption reaching record levels in the first half of the nineteenth century. Particularly bacchanalian sights were common around the Glasgow Fair in mid-July and Hogmanay (New Year's Eve), but the condemnation of Glasgow's whole pub-entertainment culture that followed ignored the fact that this was the only cultural expression most workers had access to, however loud and excessive it might have seemed to middle-class sensibilities. The 1840s saw the rapid development of a thriving temperance movement in Scotland, with its base of operations in Glasgow. While this may have attracted its fair share of bigots who viewed alcoholism as a Catholic plague and who used the movement to propose legislation aimed at further suppressing and stifling this already downtrodden community, the temperance societies of Glasgow were mostly made up of genuinely inspiring and enlightened individuals from both Protestant and Catholic faiths. In fact, rather than condemning music along with the drinking that usually accompanied it, many Glasgow temperance societies encouraged it as a means to a spiritual awakening and a cure from the grip of alcoholism.

Of course, this was not the earthy music of the pub, but church music. Participation in massed choral singing was seen as a powerful musical/spiritual experience through which drinkers could find the God-given strength to stay away from alcohol. Children were also targeted by the new evangelical teetotallers with the formation of the Band of Hope. This was a youth club centred on musical performance, at whose gatherings youngsters were taught tearjerkers about the woes of alcohol abuse such as 'The Drunkard's Raggit Wean', a tale in song guaranteed to rack any reveller with guilt. Its last verse goes:

> Oh! pity the wee laddie, sae guileless an' sae young,
> The oath that lea's the faither's lips 'ill settle on his tongue;
> An' sinfu' words his mither speaks his infant lips 'ill stain,
> For, oh! There's nane to guide the bairn, the drunkard's raggit wean!
> Then surely we micht try an' turn that sinfu' mither's heart,
> An' try to get the faither to act a faither's part,
> An' mak them lea' the drunkard's cup, an' never taste again,
> An' cherish, wi' a parent's care, their puir wee raggit wean.

The temperance movement resulted in a number of steps, some helpful and some less so, taken to combat alcoholism. The more enlightened proposals saw attractive alternatives to the pub established, such as a St. Patrick's Day musical soirée held at Glasgow held in City Hall in 1844, while less thought-out steps included legislation targeting pubs themselves, the most well-known of which was the Forbes-Mackenzie Act of 1853. This closed Scottish pubs on Sundays and introduced an 11 pm closing time. The main effect of this Act was a boom in illegal drinking dens known as shebeens, at which home-distilled spirits were served and lively music played. The whisky at these places was a sort of wicked raw spirit, not the refined malts whisky Scotland is famous for today. Another damaging effect of the 1853 licensing laws was the reinforcement of stale Glasgow stereotypes: of a dour Protestant elite who wanted everyone in church or at work and a Catholic proletariat that was hell-bent on the satisfaction of worldly appetites. The same divisions within Glasgow would be flushed out by other forms of popular entertainment in the coming decades; there was a movement against going to the cinema in the early 1900s, as well as strong feeling against the thriving Italian ice-cream trade.

The movement against alcohol coincided with the arrival of a sort of musical compromise between the pub sessions and the church choir. Music hall had grown out of the 'free and easies' of the first half of the century, offering an evening of music, comedy and dance performances for all the family. Music hall was effective in attracting audiences from across the social spectrum, and so was less susceptible to, although not immune from, the disapproval of what labour journalist Thomas Johnston called 'the social purity humbugs'. The rise of music hall, together with the growing taste for theatre – in part due to the increase in Jewish European immigration in the second half of the nineteenth century – saw an astonishing period of theatre and music-hall construction in Glasgow. This theatre phase coincided with the period when Glasgow was the world's greatest shipbuilding centre, which lasted up until 1918. In her chronicle of Glasgow's cultural life, *Social Sculpture*, Sarah Lowndes notes that 'between 1862 and the outbreak of the Great War, 18 major theatres were built in Glasgow'. Although Glasgow's great theatres and music halls had a tendency to burn down or be demolished, some of them have survived to this day, although not often in their original guises. Some of them, such as the Britannia Music Hall in the Trongate, now exist as bingo halls, while others, such as the Coliseum on Eglington Street, were converted into cinemas. Sadly, the Coliseum now stands disused, a strange sight when compared with its next-door neighbour, the thriving Carling Academy, which started life as the Bedford Theatre.

5.
BEDROOM HEADLINERS

t was a dark and stormy night. Not a particularly good night for an outdoor pop concert.

The year ahead might have looked good for Franz Ferdinand, but the night ahead did not look rosy for musicians attempting a celebratory outdoor show. Especially those intending to use a high-voltage public-address system. On this particular Hogmanay, those about to rock could expect to get very wet.

Edinburgh's *Concert in the Gardens* has become the centrepiece of the city's world-famous Hogmanay celebrations. The show takes place in Princes Street Gardens, a dramatic venue with the castle looming on the crag above on one side and Sir Walter Scott's gothic memorial peering down from Princes Street on the other. The one major weak point – one that gets worse every year and which has been bemoaned by the many frustrated Edinburgh Festival promoters who use the Gardens during the summer (but still face unpredictable Scottish weather) – is the Ross Bandstand. This large, outdoor stage is used throughout the year for music and theatre in the heart of Edinburgh. Unfortunately, it is a temporary-style structure that is left up all-year-round to face the battering of the Scottish weather.[5] On New Year's Eve 2003-4, with Franz due to play on the rickety structure (kicking the show off for the Coral and Erasure), 70 mph winds were in the process of ripping pieces off the stage's canopy. A large volume of water was making its way through the resulting holes and onto the stage – where all the wires, PA systems, lights and other pieces of equipment required to put on a pop concert were getting drenched.

As the clouds gathered over Edinburgh, a crisis meeting took place. Picture the scene: with the wind whistling about outside and the rain

5. It might seem like madness to hold an outdoor concert in December in Scotland, but Edinburgh's weather is actually much drier than Glasgow's. Average annual rainfall between 1971 and 2000 for Glasgow was 1205.3 mm, with Edinburgh getting just over half of that at 676.2 mm (UK Met Office).

lashing against the window panes, the noble elders of Edinburgh [6] tugged beards and searched consciences. Should they – nay, could they – cancel one of the world's premier New Year's celebrations? Gloomy technical reports were delivered stating that the already decrepit bandstand had been seriously damaged by the wind, that the integrity of the whole structure was threatened, and that the damage was leading to ever 'greater water ingress' onto the stage. Experts also opined that the rockets of the famous Seven Hills Fireworks Display were likely to be hurled into chaotic trajectories by the high winds battering the city.

Visions of rain, mud, high-voltages, collapsing stages and horizontal fireworks cutting through the crowd combined in the minds of the concert organisers and sponsors to paint a picture of the mother of all midnight medieval battles. And so the show was called off.

Much of the blame for this state of affairs has been laid at the door of Edinburgh's City Council, who own the Ross Bandstand and rent it out to promoters. To be fair to them, in the light of the Hogmanay fiasco, the Council flew into action and put forward plans to replace the old structure with a new, larger and more permanent building. Sadly, they then came up against a piece of their own legislation passed in 1991 that prohibits any further building in Princes Street Gardens. The Scottish Executive told them it would take about two years to get the legislation changed. So future Hogmanay concert performers still face the same uncertain fate that Franz faced at the dawn of 2004.

If there is one thing Franz Ferdinand are good at, though, it's finding alternative venues. Much of their early career in Glasgow was based on the practice of seeking out unusual places to perform and so avoid the merry-go-round of the same old, tired old venues. While the other Hogmanay bands took the night off and the crowds filtered into Edinburgh's pubs or just went home, Franz set about finding a friendly local with a space they could perform in. It didn't take long. Alex asked his younger sister, who was studying at Edinburgh at the time, and she soon discovered a friend of a friend was having a house party and would of course love to have Franz Ferdinand playing a concert in his bedroom.

6. Noble elders: Lothian and Borders Police, City of Edinburgh Council, Unique Events, safety advisers, Royal Bank of Scotland (sponsors).

As soon as the arrangements had been made, the lucky party giver, Malcolm Jack, later to be Music Editor for Edinburgh's *Fest* magazine, set about converting his humble abode in the Marchmont area of Edinburgh just south of the historic centre into a music venue capable of housing Scotland's hottest new band. It wasn't just a matter of moving sofas, however, as the band's equipment was still in the Ross Bandstand, which was now officially out of bounds. Between 9.30 pm, when the new arrangements were made, and 12.15 am, when Franz launched into 'Cheating On You', replacement equipment was tracked down and installed in Malcolm's bedroom – including a single microphone held together with Sellotape.

From their expected audience of 100,000, Franz could have been forgiven for feeling slightly miffed that they ended up playing to about 50 people crammed into a suburban semi. Despite the makeshift PA system, Franz performed their set with their usual high energy and soon had their audience dancing along. It was a typical Franz moment, and one that the band had the wisdom to appreciate. Already, they could see that the year ahead was to have them propelled into the stratosphere of the pop world, so to start the year playing to an audience of 50 people, many of them family and friends, would have been refreshingly down to earth. By the end of the year, Franz would have performed the same songs to hundreds of thousands.

6.
DOLE DANCING

The First World War marked the end of Glasgow's great period of shipbuilding prosperity. For the many thousands in the crowded tenement blocks in areas such as Partick, Greenock, Ibrox and Clydebank, into which extra workers were being crammed to meet the needs of the wartime production, the so-called period of prosperity had long been a joke. Worse still, unscrupulous landlords took advantage of the housing shortage to instigate rent hikes, which most of the tenants could not afford. At the same time, the working classes in Glasgow were becoming increasingly politicised, with the steady growth of the labour movement and support for the Independent Labour Party. The combination of economic downturn, the growing self-identification of the working class as a group worthy of rights, and the continuing pressure from landlords resulted in the rent strikes of 1915, in which Glasgow's women were the driving force. The strikes were extremely effective, and within the year the Liberal Government, faced with the prospect of further industrial crises hindering the war effort, introduced rent restrictions.

The success of the rent strikes proved to be an inspiration to workers throughout the city, many of whom had already begun to take action against conditions and pay. This was the period known as Red Clydeside, in which socialist ideals flourished and workers staged a series of mass strikes. The economic decline continued, however, and workers were laid off in their thousands. By 1922, some 90,000 were out of work. The one-time industrial giant of the world was mortally wounded, although it would struggle on for five decades.

Economic disaster, housing crises and mass unemployment did not get in the way of young Glaswegians' appetite for entertainment, however. The early twentieth century saw the growth of three forms of entertainment in Glasgow: football, cinema and dancing. By 1940, Glasgow had over 120 cinemas – more per head than any city outside the USA, and 93 Palais de Danse – more per head than any city anywhere in the world. The most famous and enduring of the Glasgow dance halls were the Locarno, Barrowland Ballroom, Green's Ballroom, the Albert, the Berkeley and Dennistoun Palais. As we'll see, these halls were to become the cradle of the city's pop music scene.

From the beginning of the century until well into the 1960s, dance halls were the place where Glasgow's young could hear and dance to the latest music. Record imports from the USA, where all the new music was coming from, were relatively rare and hard to get hold of. The dance bands that catered for younger audiences – as opposed to those aimed at their parents – would try to get hold of whatever new songs they could and provided a sort of live juke box service for their audiences. Even for these musical scouts, however, sounds travelled slowly across the Atlantic and the standard repertory remained fairly staid. Even so, the dance halls were the first regular meeting places for young people en masse in Glasgow, and provided soil for the growth of the youth subcultures that would flourish after the Second World War.

During the 1930s, a musical sensation was occurring in America – one that was a precursor of the rock 'n' roll explosion of the 1950s. Manhattan had become the centre of a new, faster, dancier expression of jazz. Duke Ellington had set the foundations during his band's residence at the Cotton Club, and Cab Calloway received the baton at the same venue when Ellington embarked on a world tour in 1930. In January 1934, Cab Calloway recorded 'Jitterbug', the title of which would be applied to a style of dancing that was about to sweep the nation. Black dance styles such as the Lindy and Shag had been developing for a while at the Savoy Ballroom, but were restricted to a relatively small and mostly black in-crowd. It was white musician and bandleader Benny Goodman who took the energised musical styles of the Manhattan scene and packaged them for white America. His radio show 'National Biscuit Saturday Night', broadcast the sound of the Harlem hotspots right across the country. When he took his band on tour in 1934, Goodman found that the West Coast kids in particular had been tuning in and getting into the East Coast sound. His tour's arrival in California prompted the start of the Jitterbug era. The word was a general label applied to all the black-style dancing that was now becoming a hit in ballrooms across the country.

While music can be recorded and exported, a style of dancing is more difficult to replant in another country. In 1942, however, America entered the Second World War and thousands of US soldiers were shipped over to Britain. It was a cultural invasion on a massive scale, albeit one that most of the locals couldn't get enough of. Nowhere was the presence of the young Americans felt more than in the dance halls. They brought with them the music and dance styles that had by now become a national craze in the States. Soon, jitterbugging had caught on across Britain, despite occasional attempts to stop it – some dance-hall managers put up notices stating 'No Jitterbugging'. With its super-fluity of dance venues, the impact on Glasgow was particularly marked, strengthening an already strong cultural link with the States for which the shipbuilding and shipping industries had long been the lifeline. And of course, with their almost equal love of the cinema, Glaswegians had already developed a strong taste for US popular culture through its movies. Glasgow's wartime love affair with jazz endured, and jazz remains a strong part of the city's musical character to this day. Speaking of love affairs, the link was also strengthened by the large numbers of 'GI brides' who left for America with their new husbands at the end of the war.

As well as black music and black dancing, the war also brought real, flesh-and-blood black Americans to Britain in larger numbers than ever before. Unlike in the States, where segregation was still the prevailing policy in the South, black American soldiers were largely viewed by the British public as being on an equal footing with their white counter-parts. In fact, as the craze for jitterbugging took hold, they were seen as something of an exotic and exciting import – the genuine article as far as the new music style was concerned. Civil-rights writer Roi Ottley was sent to Britain as a war correspondent, and reported on the impact of black American soldiers on the British public: 'The Negro has brought along his gifts. I was quite surprised to find British girls in Manchester, Liverpool, Glasgow and London dancing the lindy hop.'

Reinvigorated by the American invasion, the Glasgow dance-hall scene flourished during and after the war, despite the city's continuing industrial slow down, unemployment and housing problems. It seemed that the worse things got, the more Glasgow's youth wanted to dance and listen to music. Things were not all fun and games, however. The dance halls were also a hangout for the many gangs that were forming in the environment of unemployment and civic malaise. Wielding their chosen weapons, usually razor blades – known locally as a 'malky' or 'chib' – gangs would often use dance halls as venues for turf battles. Some venues were forced to close after a series of such confrontations. One of the styles most associated with the gangs in Britain in the 1950s was the teddy boy look. The distinctive style of clothing, which had originated from Savile Row as an expression of wealth for well-off young men-about-town, was picked up by the spivs of London's East End as the epitome of cool (in much the same way as the Burberry tartan has recently become synonymous with the 'chav' look – known as 'neds' in Glasgow). Named after the Edwardian period that it evokes, the teddy boy look consisted of drain-pipe trousers, a long jacket with large lapels and no waist, suede shoes, bright socks and long hair (long for the period, anyway). The look caught on in Glasgow, and became the first distinctive youth subculture. It also became synonymous with a rebellious outlook and appetite for violence – a reputation that meant that many dance halls banned anyone dressing in teddy boy style outright.

At the same time, another musical sensation was brewing in America, a new style that would mark the beginning of the modern era of pop music. Black American musicians continued to be a crucial creative force in American popular music, but the race divide meant that it was still viewed simply as black music for black people – it was labelled 'race music' in record shops – and was only reaching a relatively small white audience. A series of marketing strategies were called into play to make white ears open to black music. The first was the coining of the name 'Rhythm and Blues' in 1947 by Jerry Wexler, then writing for *Billboard* magazine and soon to become a groundbreaking producer. This simple act of classification meant that the music could start appearing in the *Billboard* charts as a class of its own, without the tag of 'race music'.

This was an important first step, and a larger and larger white audience was indeed finding its way to R&B, but a further act of processing was required to win America over to black music. In 1951, a DJ called Alan Freed was hosting a music programme aimed at a young audience on WJW Radio in Cleveland, Ohio. Local record shop owner Leo Mintz alerted him to the fact that there was a craze among his young, white clientele for black music – R&B. In response, Freed came up with a new show to cater for this emerging market. Instead of sticking with the term Rhythm and Blues, however, he came up with a new name that wasn't lumbered with any black image that might have stopped his white audience tuning in. The name he came up with was Rock and Roll. His new show, *Moondog's Rock and Roll Party*, pumped out solid R&B tracks to his existing audience. And they loved it. In fact, they loved it so much that *Moondog* soon had a huge following. Eager to capitalise on his new R&B disciples, Freed arranged for a concert, the grandiosely named *Moondog's Coronation Ball*, to be held in Cleveland Arena in March 1953. In the event, the crowds that turned up were just too huge and the ball had to be cancelled. What was striking, though, was that in the supposedly segregated city, both white and black kids had turned up. In 1954, Freed was poached by WINS New York to bring his musical revolution to the Big Apple. Within just a few months of being on the air, Freed's show, now called *The Big Beat*, had made WINS the biggest station on the East Coast.

Just because people were listening to R&B and calling it rock 'n' roll didn't mean that it wasn't still R&B. What became rock 'n' roll music began when white musicians tried to combine R&B with what they were already playing. This was precisely what Bill Haley did. He and his Saddlemen had started out as a country band. In 1951, while Alan Freed was peddling R&B to white kids in Cleveland, Bill Haley tried something similar by recording a version of 'Rocket 88', an R&B song originally by Jackie Brenston and His Deltacats. Many other white bands at the time were also engaging these cross-over experiments. Following on from this success, Haley changed the band's name to the Comets to get away from the country image and, over the next four years, recorded some of the first bona fide rock 'n' roll songs: 'Rock The Joint' (1952), 'Crazy, Man, Crazy' (1953), 'Rock Around the Clock' (1954) and 'Shake, Rattle and Roll' (1955) – most of them covers of R&B originals. Bill Haley might have sounded the starting gun, but it was those that followed who ensured that rock 'n' roll was no passing fad: Elvis Presley, Jerry Lee Lewis, Chuck Berry, Buddy Holly and Little Richard the foremost among them.

The rock 'n' roll revolution first landed in Glasgow in 1956, not in the dance halls this time, but in the cinema. *Blackboard Jungle* was the first rock 'n' roll film, aimed at a teenage audience and dealing with High School rebellion. It also opened with 'Rock Around the Clock'. The potent mixture of rebels and rock 'n' roll bowled young British audiences over. As the film opened around the country, there were reports of riots, seat-slashing and outbreaks of dancing in the aisles. In Glasgow, as Sarah Lowndes describes in *Social Sculpture*, 'residents were shocked when hundreds of teddy boys and girls danced in Keith Street outside the Tivoli Cinema, Partick after a screening of the film'. This joyful reception can be seen as just one moment in Glasgow's long love affair with American music. What is special about this particular moment, however, is that for the first time there was a style of music that belonged specifically to the young and that tacitly encouraged them to pick up a guitar and do it themselves. And they did.

7.
THE RIDE BEGINS

Peering ahead into 2004, Nick, Alex, Bob and Paul could have been forgiven for feeling exhilarated... and just a little bit apprehensive. The New Year had coincided with a point that saw the band just teetering on the edge of the rollercoaster of pop success; they had slogged their way uphill thus far, and now the thrill ride was about to begin. But their progress on the track ahead was not absolutely certain. Could they keep the momentum going sufficiently to take the double loops of European success and, crucially, ride out the corkscrew of American acclaim? Record companies are always on the lookout for that golden egg, the global act – a pop act that can get feet tapping in the UK, Europe, America and Asia. Oasis, for example, were giants of the UK market, but floundered in the States. At the beginning of 2004, UK success for Franz Ferdinand seemed to be in the bag, but whether the rest of the world would follow nobody could tell. This was the make-or-break year for Franz Ferdinand. The debut album was recorded, tour dates were being booked, and now the band had to show the world that the rave press was not just hype. Over the next 12 months, the band would perform over 200 shows in 22 different countries, their debut album and three singles would be released through Domino and their faces would be seen on magazine covers around the world. By the following December, Franz would know exactly how big a band they were destined to be.

The combined effect of Alex's experience and knowledge of the music press, together with the guiding input of manager Cerne Canning and the PR genii at Domino had already helped them to catch the attention of the UK pop rags – not forgetting that promotional outtakes from the album were doing the rounds and creating a huge amount of buzz, as was a supposedly unofficial bootleg recording of a concert in Amsterdam, subsequently given official release as part of the Limited Edition of the first album. It seemed that the sound Franz were purveying was just what the hacks had been waiting for: it was indie, but it was pop; it was completely of the moment, yet it contained within it a short history of the last forty years of popular music; clubbers could dance to it, and music nerds could analyse the influences within it. It was just the sort of thing that the *NME* especially feels comfortable getting behind: not too commercial, not too highbrow.

If a band's success can be measured by its initial reception in the music press, then Franz Ferdinand were going to be huge. The *NME*, always desperately seeking the Next Big Thing to back, made Franz the cover story for the first issue of the year. There was nothing extraordinary about the article itself, which featured an interview with the band, but the strapline used to accompany the cover image was a little out of the ordinary. It seemed that Franz could now count on the UK's premier pop journal to be on their side; the *NME* might have won itself a reputation for some spectacular u-turns in the past (it's take on Radiohead, for example, has swung violently pro and con), but it would be difficult to take back a statement as hyperbolic as 'This Band Will Change Your Life'.

It was a great start to the year for Franz. It also prepared the ground as well as they could have hoped for the release of their first single of the year, the second in all, 'Take Me Out'. The decision to make 'Take Me Out' the second rather than the first release was a piece of marketing genius. While 'Darts of Pleasure', released the previous September, had provided ample fuel for the growing media frenzy, 'Take Me Out' was launched at just the right moment to take the band into another level of public awareness. Clearly the strongest contender for a single on the album – with its perfectly timed slowdown and bridge one minute in, followed by a dramatic gear shift into a driving, thumping dance beat offset by a simple but gloriously catchy guitar riff – the song was the perfect vehicle with which to launch Franz Ferdinand's bid for global success.

Their success over the coming year would be thanks in no small part to the irresistible, head-nodding rhythm and riff at the heart of 'Take Me Out'. This was acknowledged by Alex in January 2005, when he took part in a discussion at the University of Edinburgh's Reid Hall about the role of Scotland in twenty-first century music. As an introduction to his speech, Alex reported that the rest of the band had suggested that the only reason he had been invited was that 'na na na na na na na was a catchy tune'. He then added, 'but then again, that's a good enough reason for me to be here tonight.' After all, pop music, from Chuck Berry to Kraftwerk, is the story of thumping rhythms and catchy tunes – and 'Take Me Out' had both.

The CD edition of the single also featured a slow, stripped-out version of the first single, 'Darts of Pleasure' re-named 'Words So Leisured', as well as a new song, 'All For You, Sophia'. The latter was an attempt to play with the last words of the band's namesake, the Archduke Franz Ferdinand, before his death by an assassin's bullet (the assassin's name was Gavrilo Princip, also mentioned in the lyric). In the song, instead of addressing his wife Sophia, the Archduke issues a sado-masochistic come-on to Gavrilo Princip – 'Shoot me, Gavrilo' – before commenting that 'Europe's going to weep', a reference to the First World War, which the assassination sparked. This misguided exploration of early twentieth-century history only went to show how strong 'Take Me Out' was – it simply didn't matter what was on the rest of the disc. The seven-inch stuck to safer territory, with an acoustic version of the album track 'Auf Achse', re-named 'Truck Stop'. The single was accompanied by a striking video that would go on to win acclaim and awards. Following the strong typographical and design identity already established on the band's cover art, the 'Take Me Out' video featured an animated collage of disembodied limbs and mechanical parts, all thumping and pumping to the driving beat of the song. 'We wanted it to be like a Dada-ist photomontage, where perspective's jumbled up and there's a strange jerkiness',[7] Alex explained to the *Daily Telegraph*.

'Take Me Out' was released on Monday, 12 January. By the following Wednesday, the midweek UK chart registered it at Number Two; by the end of the week and the official Chart positions on Sunday it had slotted in at Number Three, behind *Pop Idol* winner Michelle McManus's 'All This Time' and Harlem diva Kelis's comeback hit, the ever-so-blandly naughty 'Milkshake'. There was a bitter irony in McManus's triumph; Franz had been pipped by a Glasgow girl whose act was a product of the Simon Fuller *Pop Idol* conveyor belt – a musical phenomenon that represented everything Franz stood against.

There was little time to ponder such twists of fate, however, as the touring had already begun. Franz had already been over to Holland for Groningen's small but influential Eurosonic Festival. Following the 'Take Me Out' release, the band made the first of six visits to the States that year, to play at a relatively new but already hip venue in Williamsburg,

7. Craig McLean, *Daily Telegraph*, Arts, 13 December 2003.

Brooklyn called Northsix. (Many of the shows early in 2004 were now looking slightly small for Franz's rapidly increasing shoe size.) The band returned to the UK for their first appearance on *Top of the Pops* on 23 January. Although they were already focusing on global success, making it onto TOTP was an important moment for the band, especially for Alex, who remembered that 'my mum and dad got me a red plastic guitar and I used to jump up and down with it whenever the show was on.'[8] As with the defeat of 'Take Me Out' in the chart by Michelle McManus, Franz's first TOTP appearance would prove to be a brush with manufactured pop. They appeared after Alex Parks, the 2003 winner of *Fame Academy*, and before a video of Britney Spears in Japan. It was a powerful moment, as it showed Franz Ferdinand in their new context – not just another UK indie guitar band, but champions of homemade pop songs in an industry that had long taken that weighty responsibility in-house. As Alex stamped along to the driving rhythm, it was as if he were making a profound point that required the punctuation of his foot slamming onto the floor. 'Take Me Out' was fast becoming an anthem for the growing campaign for real music, and the bookends of Alex Parks and Britney Spears only highlighted the peril that the music industry was descending into.

The *NME* Awards Tour kicked off on 25 January in Newcastle. It proved to be an invigorating experience for Franz, as the clamorous response of the audiences fed their appetite for energetic performance. Franz were positioned bottom of the bill beneath the Von Bondies, The Rapture, and Funeral For A Friend. At the same time as Franz were opening shows on the *NME* Tour, they were also making final arrangements for their own forthcoming headline tour of the UK. Still, the *NME* Tour was a useful start to the year, and had a history of launching bands to wider recognition. The only problem was that Franz were starting to get more recognition than some of the other bands higher up on the running order, and the successful sales of 'Take Me Out', together with the increasing media clamour around the band, meant that this order began to look out of kilter. Relations with the other bands didn't suffer though, and Franz teamed up with the Von Bondies to play a private show for the *Dazed And Confused* magazine party at the Regency Hotel in London on 5 February. The *NME* Tour's final date was Cardiff University on 8

8. Tim Barr, 'Franz Ferdinand and the Art of Parties', *PlayMusic*, March 2004.

February, and *Franz Ferdinand*, the album, was launched the next day. The manic schedule that would take over most of the year was already gearing up: from Cardiff, the band returned to Glasgow for an in-store set in Virgin Megastore and then set off for London for an appearance in HMV on Oxford Street. Sales at these in-store events were impressive and proved to set the nationwide trend. The album followed the fate of 'Take Me Out': arriving at Number Two midweek before settling at Number Three for the official round-up at the weekend. When you consider that the two acts ahead of Franz were Norah Jones and Katie Melua, Number Three becomes an even more impressive result.

Now, with the album out, it was time to hit the road and sell it. The next date in the tour diary was the start of a US mini-tour to begin in the faded grandeur of the Bowery Ballroom in downtown Manhattan, but before that Franz took a trip to London to another 1920s pleasure palace, the Hammersmith Palais, to pick up an *NME* Philip Hall Radar Award. This gong goes to the British act judged by the *NME* to be the hottest new thing of the year, but, with Franz Ferdinand already riding high in the singles and album charts, the award came a little too late to be thought of as particularly prescient.

Franz Ferdinand's second trip of 2004 to the States was their first chance to really make an impact on American audiences. Although not a major tour, it was just enough to plant the seed in the hip circles of the East Coast and Canada. The New York show at the Bowery Ballroom was an important hurdle to clear – not only would the response of the 550-strong audience set the tone for the rest of the tour, but the crowd contained a large proportion of A&R men from major labels all looking to court the Glasgow foursome. Franz were left in no doubt that this was to be an audition for the American music industry when gifts of Dom Perignon champagne and knitted sweaters started piling up (it was still very cold in New York that February). Franz Ferdinand had already shown that they were not a group to be bowled over by the lavish excesses of the industry, nor were they likely to jump into bed with the first major that sent them flowers and the promise of millions. For one thing, the band were knowledgeable enough about the music industry to be aware that that initial payments from record companies were advances on future royalties, not just free cash. Commenting on the Hives' reported payment of in the region of $10 million to sign to a US label, Nick told *Q* magazine 'Don't bands know it's a loan. They'll never pay that back. It ends up being just another job.'

The Bowery show was the easy bit. The following days were filled with hours of interviews with the American press, with Alex exhausting even his bountiful supply of comment, self-analysis and soundbite. With the interviews complete, Alex, Nick and Bob took the ferry over the Hudson to Hoboken, leaving Paul in bed with 'flu. Hoboken is the home of the famous Water Music studios where the band had booked time to record tracks to accompany the forthcoming single, 'Matinée'. The result was a set of intriguing acoustic recordings, including versions of album tracks 'Jacqueline' (renamed 'Better In Hoboken') and '40''. The recordings reveal Nick McCarthy's classical and experimental jazz background as he takes to the double bass with considerable flair.

With successful shows in Canada and finally Boston and Philadelphia, Franz returned to the UK with their task complete – the seed had been planted and the press were clamouring for more. The return to the UK brought an enjoyable 'Jim'll Fix It' moment for Alex and Paul, as they were invited to host an hour-long show on BBC Radio 1, filling in for indie angel Steve Lamacq. For Franz fans, it was an opportunity to gain an insight into the music that made the band tick. Amid a liberal sprinkling of their own songs, the band played numbers by some key influences, including The Fall, Duran Duran, Sparks, The Smiths, the B-52s, Brian Eno and the Monochrome Set.

A brief sojourn on Scottish soil was soon interrupted by another tour. This time, Franz were off to Europe to build on the progress they had made in 2003. The tour took in Holland, Belgium, Germany and Italy. Meanwhile, things were brewing in the States. Having made a positive impact on the record industry scouts at the Bowery Ballroom, Franz were now being courted by a number of major US labels for the license to distribute their material in America.

The eventual winner of this bidding war was the mighty Sony BMG Music Entertainment, one of whose labels, Epic, made the official purchase. Epic had been a CBS label started in the 1950s to put out jazz and classical recordings, before it started to move into rock, R&B and country in the 1960s. Its heyday came in the 1980s and 1990s, when artists such as Michael Jackson, Luther Vandross, Ozzy Osborne and Céline

Dion produced a sequence of platinum-selling records. It was gobbled up by Sony, along with the rest of CBS, in 1988, before Sony itself was partially digested by German media giant Bertelsmann in a merger negotiated in 2003. To many in the indie scene, the name Sony is the very epitome of commercialised music, and therefore perhaps a strange choice for a band who saw themselves as champions of real music and who chose Domino Recording Co Ltd because it still bore the personal touch of founder and director Laurence Bell. The Japanese electronics giant Sony, working with the Dutch company Philips, had developed and introduced CDs in the late 1970s and early 1980s, and had pioneered the digital recording revolution. Its take on the music industry, therefore, has always been as a source of content for its discs. Sony technicians refer to music as 'software' – in other words, it's simply the stuff that goes on the CDs. By the turn of the millennium, the digital revolution had turned sour on the music industry. Music reduced to binary code had become a slippery fish when it came to controlling copyright and illegal duplication, especially with the growth of the Internet. Sony's technological triumphs of two decades ago were quickly becoming a huge liability to both it and the entire music industry. The crisis continues to unfold, and it was Sony's declining music sales that led it into the arms of Bertelsmann. The worry for bands signed to electronics giants such as Sony that happen to run music divisions to provide content for their discs is that they don't understand the music business. This is an issue raised by Ed Bicknell, the manager of 1980s soft rock giants and CD promo act Dire Straits, who reports, 'Alain Levy said to me when he left PolyGram, one of the problems he had was that the Philips board did not understand the business. That's true of Sony, AOL and Bertelsmann.'[9]

If signing to Epic lays Franz Ferdinand open to accusations of 'selling out' from the indie community, then the band could do worse than to employ the 'Clash defence'. After they had signed to Epic in 1977, the Clash – whose entire *raison d'être* was tied up with raising two fingers to the system – faced a barrage of abuse from fans who felt they had been betrayed. At one US show, singer Joe Strummer answered the vociferous hecklers screaming 'sell-out' by quipping, 'Well, if we hadn't signed with

9. Louis Barfe, *Where Have All The Good Times Gone*, p. 334.

CBS none of you lot would have heard of us.' [10] The Clash's decision to sign with Epic would have many unforeseen consequences, not least of which was that their presence on the Epic roster was what guided the highly politicised 1990s band Rage Against The Machine to sign with the label. The band's guitarist Tom Morello would later affirm Strummer's statement by insisting that if the Clash hadn't signed with Epic, he would not have heard of them and his musical education would have taken a very different direction. [11] In this light, it could be argued that if Franz Ferdinand had to sign with a global major, then it might as well be through the acceptable portal of Epic, with its history of signing bands uncomfortable with the idea of 'selling out'.

How much time Franz Ferdinand had to ponder these issues is debatable; as the bidding war reached its climax, they were still safely on the road in Europe, where the final date took them to Bologna in Italy to take part in an evening of music hosted by local record label Homesleep on Saturday 13 March. The following Monday, the band would be in Los Angeles for the start of their next US tour. Before they jetted over the Atlantic, however, Franz had a strange, once-in-a-lifetime job to do in London.

Morrissey, the lyric writer and singer of the Smiths, was staging a spectacular comeback after a decade in the wilderness. Having become alienated from the London record labels, the music press and the other ex-Smiths, Morrissey had exiled himself in Los Angeles for six years. Out of the blue came another solo album, which Morrissey would release through the Attack label of Sanctuary Records. Although he needed to get the coverage of the *NME* for the launch of the album in May, Morrissey did not want to deal directly with the magazine after a snubbing he had received some years before. The compromise that was reached was that Franz would interview Morrissey and the resulting encounter would be printed in the *NME*. The magazine would get its story of the comeback of the year, Morrissey would get his coverage, and Franz would get to talk to one of their musical heroes for an hour or two. In fact, the Mancunian singer had already showed his interest in Franz by asking them to sup-

---

10. Quoted from John Street, *Rebel Rock*, p. 144, in turn quoting from G. Burn, 'Good Clean Punk', *Sunday Times Magazine*, date unknown.

11. Tom Morello, 'The Clash and Joe Strummer', audioslavica.com.

port his homecoming concert in Manchester in May. The interview was an extremely shrewd move by Morrissey – he was taking on the role of the senior popster championing the young hopefuls Franz Ferdinand. In fact, the growing hype surrounding Franz would be sure to rub off on him and would show that he still had his finger on the musical pulse. The band could have been forgiven for feeling some trepidation at the prospect of extracting interesting comment from the ex-Smiths singer: he had developed a reputation as one of the most challenging interviewees in the world of pop. The fateful meeting took place in a Paddington hotel, and Morrissey was ... charming, relaxed and gently witty. In fact, much of Morrissey's comeback has been marked by surprised pundits commenting on the fact that the singer appears – dare they use the word – happy. The resulting interview between Franz, Morrissey and a representative of the *NME* was published over two issues in May 2004. Perhaps as a gesture of thanks and to reaffirm their commitment to the Franz cause, the *NME* would publish another cover story on the band at the end of March.

With the album released in the States, a deal done with Epic (including an advance reportedly in the region of $1.5 million), and the media hungrier than ever for a band that was shaping up to be huge, Franz Ferdinand toured the USA again. This time, it was the West Coast and the South with shows in LA, San Francisco, and an important appearance at the South By Southwest Festival in Austin, Texas. This festival has long been a reliable point of entry into the American market for UK bands of an indie/rock persuasion, and has developed particularly close links of late with the Glasgow scene. The festival more or less takes over the city, as thousands of music fans and almost as many acts (over a thousand, anyway) descend on Texas (whose unofficial state motto reads: 'Texas: Bigger Than France'). A film festival, an interactive technologies conference and even a golf tournament run concurrently and add to the visitor numbers. Once again, however, Franz Ferdinand were way ahead of where they expected to be at this time in their career. The buzz around them in the States was growing, and the Buffalo Billiards venue they appeared in, which could accommodate 1500, proved somewhat too small for the crowd who wanted to see the band. Franz appeared that night along with Sons And Daughters, who were not only Domino label mates but also pals from Glasgow; their raw, honest sound was the perfect complement to Franz's upbeat pop rhythms.

8.
HOLY HARVEY

If Glasgow should ever require a patron saint of rock, there could only ever be one name on the list of candidates. Alex Harvey.

It could be argued that Alex Harvey was playing rock 'n' roll before it touched Scottish shores from the States. Throughout the 1950s, he and his friends would head out from Glasgow on a Friday night to the shores of Loch Lomond, with a bottle of whisky for sustenance. Sitting around a campfire, the group would sing the night away.[12] Songs for these excursions were precious commodities, and Alex would seek them out wherever he could, the best source being the docks where sailors came in from America every day – and where Alex worked. The music of choice for these wild camping excursions was US country and folk music (which had plenty of Scottish blood in it anyway). Alex's performances of these songs have been described by fellow Glasgow musician Bill Patrick as 'semi-wild country music', a tantalising clue that let's us know that Alex was not simply trotting the numbers out in strict adherence to the originals. He was taking country and infusing it with a bit of... well, Glaswegian. It was precisely this instinct to cross one form of music with another approach and so create something completely new that led to the birth of rock 'n' roll.

While Alex's mighty voice echoed over the waters of Loch Lomond, another Glasgow-born musician was pioneering a musical style that would take Britain and America by storm. Anthony 'Lonnie' Donegan was playing skiffle, a type of blues that had originally sprung up in the States around 1900. It's sound was characterised by the makeshift instruments used to play it, including washtubs, washboards, combs and pretty much anything else that made a good noise. In 1956, Donegan and his band had a huge hit with a cover of the Leadbelly song 'The Rock Island Line', which resided in the charts for 11 weeks in the

12. Trips to Loch Lomond remain a popular excursion for young Glasgwegians, and Country and Western music retains a loyal following, with the Grand Ole Opry south of the Clyde its principal venue.

US and the UK, reaching Number Eight in both countries. This bizarre selling of American music back to America foreshadowed the so-called British Invasion of the next decade. The British skiffle craze served as a sort of nursery for the musicians of that British Invasion: the Beatles started as a skiffle band (the Quarrymen) and Mick Jagger was in a skiffle band before the Rolling Stones.

Skiffle showed that the musical antennae of Britain were trained on America, in particular on black and country music. It also prepared the soil for rock 'n' roll and the beat boom by teaching a creed of DIY music – the essence of skiffle was people just feeling like playing and grabbing whatever was to hand. Alex Harvey caught onto the craze and set up the Kansas City Skiffle Group, also known as the Kansas City Counts. When rock 'n' roll did arrive, Alex was ready and waiting. Armed with a rebuilt Gibson he had been given by an uncle, he set about teaching himself to play the new songs that were filtering through from the States. His big break came when journalist David Gibson of the *Sunday Mail* ran a contest to find Scotland's answer to Britain's first rock 'n' roll star, Tommy Steele. The headline 'Are you Scotland's Tommy Steele?' announced the contest and, throughout April 1957, hundreds of hopefuls auditioned for the top place in a proto-Simon Fuller-type contest. Armed with his reconstructed guitar and taking time off from his work on the docks to make the auditions, Alex blasted his way through the competition to claim the title 'Scotland's Tommy Steele'. He clinched it with an energised version of Elvis Presley's 'Hound Dog'. Alex made a good story for the journalists as he was clearly from an ordinary Glasgow background, with a job on the docks and a new wife who was a cinema usherette. This was the cherry on the cake, though, as Alex's performances – as witnessed by Bill Patrick on the lakes of Loch Lomond and by thousands of future fans – were powerful to the point of scary. He took the energy and release of rock 'n' roll and took it one step further. Over the next few years, Alex toured Scotland, performing his new style of rock 'n' roll, which was already beginning to sound like the rock music he was to influence so powerfully. As mentioned earlier, rock 'n' roll was largely made up of country and rhythm and blues. Alex had long been familiar with country, but it wasn't until the end of the 1950s that he discovered R&B. The soul sound was sweeping in from the States stronger than ever before, and once again Glasgow was one of its landing points in

Britain. Alex was blown away by the music and immediately took it onboard. The result was the Alex Harvey Soul Band, which included friends Bill Patrick on sax and Jimmy Grimes on bass, and with whom Alex arrived in Hamburg in 1962, following on the heels of the Beatles, whose residence on the famous Reeperbahn had launched their career. This marks the beginning of Alex's journeyman phase, which would take him from Hamburg to Glasgow, to London, back to Glasgow and then around the world, experiencing sporadic success and failure, but always approaching his career with a powerful, almost manic energy. If Glasgow had needed a spark to get its rock scene going, in Alex Harvey it got an explosion.

The news of Alex's return from Hamburg to Glasgow caused huge excitement around the blossoming local scene. The prophet was back from the wilderness and he had something to say. One of the eager acolytes crowded into a dark basement club to hear the word of Harvey was 13-year-old Marie Lawrie, who had already started out on a career as a pop singer in local Glasgow clubs. She remembered 'There was a real anger there, a real "fuck you" sound; the sound of youth. It was amazing!' [13] One song in particular caught Marie's attention, a cover of the Isley Brother's 'Shout'. As Lulu, Marie would make the song her own, but always infused with the energy she saw could be poured into it in that Alex Harvey performance.

13. Lulu, *Lulu*.

9.
SPRINGTIME FOR FRANZ

After completing their American tour with a race across the continent from Seattle in the west, across the border to Vancouver, then south and east to a final show in Chicago, Franz Ferdinand jetted home to spend spring 2004 in the British Isles. There was now a short break worked into their hectic schedule, intended to give them time to prepare for the next major milestone in their career – a headline tour of the UK and the release of their third single, 'Matinée'. The first weekend in April saw the marriage of Paul to his fiancée, the elegant Esther.[14] For many all-male bands, the idea of a marriage in their first big year would have been completely *verboten*, to allow room for the romantic fantasies of their prepubescent female fans. Some boy bands are instructed by publicists and managers not even to mention having partners – they are always 'looking for that special someone'. Not so for Franz Ferdinand. From the start, they had made no attempt to mislead their fans about their personal relationships (not that they chose to discuss the subject at length either). This had not been due to naivety about the music industry, but rather part of their general straightforward approach, which was emphatically about the music and not the band. Even Alex's penchant for spouting opinions on everything from world politics to pop music history has never been an attempt to build a public persona for himself as the lead singer, but rather his real character and passions coming through in interviews. This approach can be seen as a legacy of the band's incubation in the Glasgow art/music scene, where it is the norm for the focus to be on the artists' work and not the artists themselves.

As Franz took a breather, they were already finding time to write new songs, looking to their second album. The relentless touring schedule was inevitably making the band slightly weary of playing the same few songs over and over, and the impulse to get some fresh sounds into their set lists was getting ever keener. Songwriting and experimenting was a constant

14. The happy couple would team up musically as well under the name Polyester to play occasional DJ sets.

process for the Nick and Alex anyway: as Alex explained to the *NME*, 'it's something that we do all the time.' Franz's shows featured constantly rearranged running orders and usually included a sprinkling of B-sides and other non-album tracks to keep audiences on their toes.

The retreat to Glasgow was a chance for the band to catch up with friends and enjoy the novelty of sleeping in their own beds. However, the work continued apace. The respite from performing was also a chance for the management team to firm up the schedule for the summer ahead. Franz Ferdinand were by now the hot new things that everyone knew about, and the major pop festivals were all eager to showcase them. From the end of May through to August, the band's diary was filling up with bookings festivals around Europe and as far afield as Australia and Japan. Perhaps closest to their hearts was July's T In The Park Festival, held at Balado in the countryside north of Edinburgh. The band's 2003 appearance here had been Franz's first festival performance, by far their biggest audience to that point, and had marked a definite gearshift in their early career. The band's affection for the festival was highlighted by their agreement to cut short their well-earned rest to film an advert for the event in central Glasgow. Fan websites were deployed to gather a throng of Franz fans for the shoot, which consisted of the band playing 'Jacqueline' while being filmed from a helicopter. When it was launched in July, the ad had a slightly unfortunate side effect for Franz Ferdinand, as it almost made the band look as if *they* were sponsored by Tennents, and not just the festival; all of which provided more ammunition for those who wanted to tar and feather the band for 'selling out'. However, with their career in a steep ascendant, these voices were becoming more and more distant and less and less important to the band.

Break over, Franz Ferdinand began their first headline tour on 12 April, supported by The Fiery Furnaces and Sons And Daughters, with two nights at Glasgow's Queen Margaret Union, one of the two student union bodies at Glasgow University.[15] Sons and Daughters were promoting their debut album, *Love The Cup*, which had been recorded the previous summer by Glasgow's favourite producer, Andy Miller, at Delgados-owned label Chemikal Underground's in-house studio

---

15. Glasgow University Union was an all-male society; Queen Margaret Union was set up in 1890 to cater for female students. Today, QMU has more members, largely due to its 900-capacity Qudos venue.

Chem19. The Fiery Furnaces were also old friends of Franz Ferdinand, both bands having supported Canadian band Hot Hot Heat's 2003 UK tour. Centred on the sometimes sparky partnership of Illinois-born brother and sister Eleanor and Matt Friedberger, the Fiery Furnaces draw on a wonderfully diverse reserve of influences to come up with music that flits gleefully from era to era between songs and even within them. Eleanor's Patti Smith-keen vocals deliver disarmingly low-key lyrics about losing dogs, walking through the Greenwich Tunnel in London, Leeds United and croquet. There was an added benefit for Alex in the choice of the Fiery Furnaces as touring partners, as he got to spend more time with Eleanor, with whom he was going out at the time.

The tour worked its way south, taking in Liverpool, Dublin, Sheffield, Nottingham, Leeds and Birmingham. At every show – all of which were sold out – Franz Ferdinand justified the faith of their fans, demonstrating that they were one of the few live acts that could get their audiences dancing. The tour coincided with the release of 'Matinée' on 19 April,[16] which raced to Number Six in the singles chart. The video that accompanied the release was a playful reference to the song's reference to 'this academic factory', with the band dressed in school uniforms and causing havoc in the classroom, and even at one point performing beneath a giant image of Terry Wogan – also referred to in the lyrics. The album was also still selling well and, with the added promotional boost of the tour, reached its platinum sales mark. Added to this, Epic released the album in the USA and Australia at the same time as 'Matinée' was launched in the UK, with Japan following in early June. The global promise of Franz Ferdinand was now being fulfilled.

Before heading over to France for a three-date tour, Franz put on a secret gig for friends and colleagues in Leeds. The show took place at Leeds' Brudenell Social Club, not a venue accustomed to showcasing acts with an album launching around the world. The advertising for the show had Franz billed as the Black Hands, which contained a clue that students of European history and the band's own history would have picked up; the Black Hand Gang was the name of the group to which Gavrilo Princip belonged when he assassinated Archduke Franz Ferdinand in Sarajevo in 1914, and it was also a name that the band had used before

16. The 19th also saw the publication of a Franz Ferdinand-edited edition of *The Guardian* G2 arts supplement.

for a 2003 show at Glasgow's Stereo. Perhaps there were a lot of students of European history in Leeds at the time: the 'secret' part of the secret gig soon evaporated and a horde of Franz fans descended on the humble venue. [17] For those who were turned away, the band thoughtfully put on a quick encore in the car park. The following night saw their official Leeds appearance, this time at the 1300-capacity Blank Canvas venue.

Following their return from France, Franz made a special trip to Derry in Northern Ireland to appear in BBC Radio One's One Big Weekend before a crowd of thousands and a sort of mini-festival feel to the proceedings. Then it was on with the UK tour, with the Fiery Furnaces and Sons And Daughters in tow. At the end of April, Alex took a brief break from the tour to put on a performance of a different kind, taking part in a discussion of the ethics and legal issues surrounding downloading music from the Internet. Held in the Playfair Library of the University of Edinburgh and hosted by the university's School of Law, the lunchtime event gave Alex a chance to express his thanks to the Internet for its part in Franz Ferdinand's success. He not only defended downloading and admitted that he did it himself, but also pointed out that the Internet had helped Franz's name spread across continents in a sort of 'global word of mouth'. This meant that when the band arrived to play gigs in the States, some of their audiences knew album songs that hadn't been released in the UK, let alone the US, and were singing along. Alex would return to the University of Edinburgh in January 2005 to discuss Scotland's musical future and to call for state investment in pop music.

As 2004 moved from spring to summer, Franz Ferdinand moved into top gear. Almost every day, more bookings were being confirmed. May saw them on stage almost every day of the month, whipping around the UK and Europe and managing to fit in a historic performance in support of Morrissey at Manchester's MEN Arena (with the interview the band had conducted with the singer published the week before in the *NME*) as well as launching into the festival season with appearances at Barcelona's Primavera and Landgraaf's (Holland) Pinkpop festivals. And that was just the start of a summer that would see Franz Ferdinand become the most celebrated band of the moment in the world.

17. Eleanor Friedberger sang backing vocals on 'Love And Destroy'.

10.

THE BEAT

he transition from traditional ballroom to pop scene in the 1950s was not an easy one, but it took place almost brutally quickly. As George Gallagher, lead singer of the most famous Glasgow band of this period, the Poets, remembers, 'the Glasgow scene developed rapidly, probably overnight...' [18] The city's ballrooms tried to keep up with the shift from dancing as the object of the evening's entertainment to the growing importance of the band playing. In the past, the band had not been the centre of attention, and most ballrooms had house bands that trotted out the standards to order. The pop boom saw the bands themselves becoming the main attraction. In the early days of the Glasgow scene, the audiences themselves weren't sure whether they wanted to just dance, just listen or both. In one infamous episode in 1957, the Ricky Barnes All Stars (Britain's first rock 'n' roll combo) and the Kansas City Counts (with Alex Harvey at the helm) were booked to play Paisley Town Hall near Glasgow. Unfortunately, the venue was an all-seater and dancing was not allowed. The young audience, high on the energy of early rock 'n' roll and not in the mood for a quiet sit-down, clashed with the stewards. A riot erupted in which many of the venue's seats were torn up. Eventually the police showed up, but they too failed to control the mob. In fact, it was only the appearance of a performer in traditional kilt and sporran whistling old Scottish airs that calmed the crowd down. This apparition was Jackie Dennis, who combined elements of music hall (in the tradition of the great Harry Lauder) with rock 'n' roll to become a sort of Elvis in a kilt. He even had two Top 30 hits with 'La Dee Dah' and 'Purple People Eater' in 1958.

Novelty acts aside, the Glasgow scene really picked up steam in the aftermath of the Beatles' phenomenal success. Liverpool, as a west-coast port, shared many of Glasgow's characteristics, including a passion for black American music. Sara Cohen describes Liverpool as 'a city of contradictions. The wealth of its past contrasts sharply with the poverty of

18. Brian Hogg, *The History of Scottish Rock and Pop.*

both past and present. Today, sites of great beauty and grandeur such as the waterfront and spacious, landscaped parks, lie in between areas of squalor and ugliness.'[19] She could be describing Glasgow, even down to the physical details of waterfront and parks. Glasgow and Liverpool also shared a largely Irish immigrant community with its traditions of music and celebration. So when the Merseybeat phenomenon exploded and the Beatles started their run of hits, Glaswegian ears were tuned in. The Beatles' impact was ensured with a four-day tour of Scotland in January 1963, followed by a single performance in Glasgow in June and a three-day tour in October. While the arrival of the Beatles on Scottish soil was musically inspirational to some, it was politically inspirational to others. Edinburgh band the Mark Five, fed up with the lack of interest the major labels showed in anything north of the border, staged a rerun of the Jarrow March of 1936, in which unemployed workers had walked from Jarrow to London in protest about their plight. The Mark Five set out to walk from Edinburgh to London as both a protest and a publicity stunt. The tactic worked and the story made it into the press. They did not even reach London before a record label, Philips' Fontana, met them in Market Harborough clutching a contract. The Mark Five duly released a single, 'Baby What's Wrong', and were swiftly dropped. The record label had simply taken advantage of the publicity created by the band, but were not willing to promote them. The whole episode sadly highlighted the status quo that the Mark Five had been protesting against – they exposed it by becoming victims of it. The guitarist and singer with the band, Manny Charlton, would go on to greater fame with Nazareth in the 1970s. As the Shadettes, the future members of Nazareth continued to develop a bitter attitude to the state of Scottish pop. Not only were bands excluded from the London-centric music industry, but many Glasgow ballroom venues had a strict music policy requiring bands to play covers of Top 40 hits. Many jobbing Glasgow bands were thus not permitted, let alone encouraged, to create their own material or approach.

Beatlemania prompted the growth of a new sort of venue. The days of the grand ballrooms were numbered, even in Glasgow where they had reigned supreme for decades. Many had already closed since their heyday in the early 1950s, as the regular dance crowds were now con-

19. Sara Cohen, *Rock Culture in Liverpool*, 1991.

tent to stay at home and watch other people dancing on television. During the 1960s, Beat clubs started to spring up. These were smaller venues, often cellar or loft spaces, and were darker and more atmospheric than the ballrooms. They were in fact more like today's clubs. Such clubs suited both the music and the Beatnik style that often went with it. In short they were cooler than ballrooms. The ballrooms did not die out altogether: there was still a need for larger venues when big acts were in town. Some were converted to suit the modern audiences, while others survived only in the form of cinemas or bingo halls.

The first Beat clubs arrived in Edinburgh, not Glasgow, and were imported by Londoners rather than locals. Brian and Paul Waldman opened Bungys at the dawn of the 1960s, which was Scotland's first Beat-style club and coffee house. Others followed, most importantly Gamp, The Place and McGoos. To go with these venues, Edinburgh also had a lively crop of bands, including the Athenians (who were the first Scottish beat group to release a single: 'You Tell Me') and the R&B influenced Boston Dexters, who had a similar repertoire to Alex Harvey's Soul Band. The fate of the Dexters is interesting in that it proved to be a template that many subsequent bands found themselves (unhappily) following. Having established a local following under the management of Brian Waldman, who had the band dress up as Chicago-style gangsters complete with blank-firing pistols, the Dexters released a number of independent singles, the most successful of which was 'Nothin's Gonna Change'. However, success in Scotland was not translating into success further afield. The singles did catch the attention of EMI label Columbia, which signed the Dexters in 1965. Sensing that they had made it, the band moved to London to be closer to the label's offices, and recorded their first major single. Sadly, at the very point when everything should have grown easy for the Dexters, they started going wrong. Columbia imposed a single on the band written by songwriters Tommy Scott and Bill Martin, themselves from north of the border. 'I've Got Something to Tell You, Baby' was a perfectly decent pop song, but it was absolutely not what the Dexters were about. They had made their name with gutsy, bluesy, black music, not the watered-down Mersey-esque sound they were being forced to adopt in the single. It was a false start that the band never really recovered from and, after another flop single, the Boston Dexters were no more. Over the coming years, this pattern of local success followed by an unsuccessful move to London and the major labels would be repeated again and again.

Meanwhile, in Glasgow, the Poets were the band of the moment. From their base of operations at the Flamingo Ballroom on Paisley Road West, they, like the Boston Dexters over in Edinburgh, built up a considerable local following. They were also like the Dexters in being one of the first Scottish bands to have a strong, cohesive image. All dressed in velvet suits with frilly shirts, the band looked sharp and played sharp, gaining a reputation as one of the tightest bands on the scene. However, it was not possible to launch an international music career from Glasgow. The only professional recording studios were those of the BBC, which were manned by technicians not trained in music production. The Poets knew that their only route to wider success was to travel to London and get signed by one of the majors. In early 1963, the band embarked on an expedition south with the aim of trying to interest EMI. Their attempt failed, and they retreated north to lick their wounds.

By chance (apparently he glimpsed them on the cover of local music rag *Beat News* in Edinburgh Airport), Andrew Loog Oldham, manager of the Rolling Stones, became interested in the Poets. Eager to build up a stable of complementary bands alongside the Stones, Oldham signed the Poets to Decca, shipped them down to London and immediately set about recording their first single, 'Now We're Thru'. It was a long way from Paisley Road West to be suddenly part of the Stones' inner circle, at the beating heart of the Swinging Sixties. At first, a creative and productive relationship with Oldham was established, perhaps because the producer/manager enjoyed the freshness of the Poets sound, which was not as obviously blues-derivative as the Stones'. The Poets were unusual among the Glasgow bands of the period for writing their own music, rather than covering American imports. Oldham gave them enough time to write songs from start to finish in the studio – a luxury the band must have appreciated considering the paucity of recording facilities in Glasgow at the time. The band followed Oldham when he set up his own label, Immediate, in 1966. Eventually, however, the inevitable happened and Oldham began to spend less time with the Poets (as well as with other Immediate artists such as Marianne Faithful, PP Arnold and Chris Farlowe) in order to devote himself to the Rolling Stones. The Poets, who had blossomed under the sunshine of Oldham's attention, now began to fade. As internal tensions grew, lead singer George Gallagher left.

11.
SUMMER OF FRANZ

he summer of 2004 was the busiest period of touring that Franz Ferdinand had yet experienced. As they embarked on their dizzying schedule, with new dates being crammed in all the time, the band had an air of giddiness about them – a mixture of disbelief and excitement that their long dreamed-of moment had come with a sense of trepidation at the daunting task ahead of them. By this point, however, still only a few months into their period of world fame, they were quickly becoming veterans of large-scale performances. Sales of the album were steadily increasingly all over the world and, soon after its release in Japan on 2 June, *Franz Ferdinand* hit the magic one million mark. It was just the sort of boost they needed to spur them on.

At the beginning of June, the band jetted off to the West Coast of America for the start of another US tour, this time playing almost a full month of dates from San Francisco to New York, ending up in Atlanta before heading back to the UK. In line with their raised status, Epic had secured Franz their first US television appearance on the Conan O'Brien show midway through the tour. They played a polished rendition of 'Take Me Out' to a television audience of millions. By now, the band had diehard fans packing out their shows, so that each performance was marked by the audience knowing the words as well as Alex and sometimes threatening to drown his own vocals out.

The band returned to the UK to make their first appearance at the Glastonbury Festival. This temporary homecoming was a triumphant and atmospheric performance, with a huge crowd gathering around the Other Stage for the Friday night slot. As in America, the crowd helped Alex along with the vocals, while fireworks erupted to create a spectacular light show to go with the music. As a marker of the power of the performance, it was enough to boost the album up 15 places in the UK chart in the following weeks. It might have felt like a final triumph, but in fact it was just the beginning of the festival season proper. The very next day, Franz were in Scheeßel, north Germany for the Hurricane Festival, the day after that in south Germany at Neuhausen ob Eck's Southside Festival... and so on through Europe and the rest of the world for the remainder of the summer.

July opened with a highlight as Franz supported the indie queen, PJ Harvey at her Lyon gig, before the band got back to their festival bashing. From France and Belgium, the band travelled to Scandinavia before briefly returning to the British Isles for Ireland's Oxegen Festival and then another triumphant homecoming, this time to Scotland's T In The Park Festival at Balado. The previous year's appearance at Balado had marked the beginning of Franz's rise to world fame, and their senior status in the billing was a startling reminder of how far they had come in so short a period of time. A hint of a shadow was cast over the band's part in the event by the fuss over their part in the Tennent's lager advertising campaign. However, the band hardly had to time to worry about such matters, busy as they were preparing for their first tour of Australia. The fortnight after T In The Park was free of performance commitments to give the band a breather and to carry out press and TV interviews. It would be the last such 'rest' – complete with the novelty of sleeping in their own beds – that the band would get for some time.

In Australia, the band met with a further warm reception, the album and 'Take Me Out' already a feature of the charts well before their arrival. From Australia, the band flew on to Japan to headline at the Fuji Rock Festival at Naeba, their Asian debut. Throughout their frantic touring, the band were still finding time to write and even record demos of new songs. Any rehearsal or studio visit would be an opportunity to try out the latest Kapranos/McCarthy composition. New songs were then tried out live in amongst their set list standards, by which method almost half of the tracks destined for the second album were aired before the year's touring was over. With songs being prepared this early on, it was not surprising that Franz thought the new album would be ready for release in the spring of 2005, rather than the autumn as it turned out.

The build-up was now also starting for the release of the next UK single, 'Michael'. Originally, the band had intended to put a new song out as the fourth single, but the decision was made by Domino to stick to the current album. Although it is understandable that Franz might have been getting tired of playing the same songs day in, day out, Domino realised that there was still gold to be mined from the debut album. To make sure the right song was picked, the band appealed to fans to let them know which track they would like released as a single. 'Michael' came back a firm favourite, and was duly selected. The band wanted to re-record the song so that it was at least a different version from the one fans were already listening to on the album, but in the event it was decided that the existing Mälmo recording was more than good enough. The band's creative frustrations were instead channelled into the making of the video to accompany the single. Shot in a club in Berlin, the video captures a fairly dark atmosphere, but otherwise outlines the story in the lyric: their friend Michael's liberation on the dance floor and transformation into a 'beautiful dance whore'. It is a sign of the naivety of much of the music press that the homoerotic overtones of the song were found newsworthy and even dangerous, claims that Alex downplayed in interviews, insisting that the song simply told the story of a good night out. The Michael of the song was Michael Kasparis, a friend from Glasgow who had been a guitarist with Foreign Radio and an occasional member of V-Twin. He appeared in the video as himself. Along with the title track, two B-side tracks were included: 'Love And Destroy' and 'Missing You'. The former had been recorded at Avatar Studios in New York with Rich Costey, the producer who would subsequently become the band's choice to record the second album.

The band had a break from touring to free them up for promotional activities in the days around the release of 'Michael' on 16 August, but then it was back on the road and back to Europe for more festivals. British fans caught up with them once again at the end of the month, when the band played the Reading and Leeds legs of the Carling Festival, notching up three performances over the two days.

Following a final European festival appearance at Bologna, the band took a few days to prepare for their next and biggest tour of the US. A month-long list of dates awaited them, with minimum time built in around shows in order to enable the band to cover as much distance as possible. Before they embarked on the US tour, however, Franz attended the Mercury Prize award ceremony in London. They had been nominated for the prize and, as the year went on and their success continued to grow, Franz had risen to joint favourites alongside the Streets. In the event, it was Franz who claimed the prize. This was a particularly important accolade for the band, being the most respected music award in indie circles. More awards would follow, but this was the one that Franz really wanted to win.

After the ceremony, they announced their intention to donate the prize money to worthy causes, including support of the Glasgow music scene.

When Franz arrived in the States, they noticed an even more enthusiastic response from audiences than the already ecstatic reception they had met with on their June tour. Alex described it to the *NME* as 'mania', the use of which word suggests that it had started to push the bounds of what was comfortable for the band. For a group that had tried to shun the usual ego projection of pop stars, it came as something of a surprise to have created 'manic' fans. While in the States, more good news reached them from Europe: the album had topped 600,000 sales in the UK and they had been nominated for four *Q* Awards: Best Song and Best Video for 'Take Me Out', Best Album and Best New Act. They eventually won Best Video.

During time out from touring, the band teamed up with San Francisco-based producer and DJ Dan Nakamura, aka The Automator. Dan was introduced to the band through his flatmate, who happened to be part of Domino's US office. Franz were familiar with Dan's work and shared his genre-defying approach to music, and were interested to see what his take would be on their sound. They recorded a version of a new song, 'Can't Stop Feeling' with him, before Alex returned the favour by providing vocals for 'The World's Gone Mad', destined to be the first single from the album *White People*, put out under Dan's band project Handsome Boy Modelling School. While 'Can't Stop Feeling' was hinted in the press to be the next UK single, it ended up unreleased, whether because of the quality of the song or the recording, or because the timing just wasn't right is not clear. Initial excitement about a Franz Ferdinand-Automator team for the next Franz album was fuelled by Dan reporting to the *NME* that he was indeed to be the producer for the second album. This must have caused some embarrassment to the band, who were still to decide on which producer to chose. In the end, the job went to Rich Costey, with whom Franz had worked at Avatar Studios on new versions of 'Love And Destroy' and the next US single, 'This Fire' (renamed 'This Fffire' to mark the difference).

After a final US show at New York's largest ballroom venue, Roseland Ballroom, and an appearance on the famous *David Letterman Show*, Franz headed home once again, buzzing with the fact that they were well on their way to becoming a major act in the USA, a feat that few European bands manage.

October saw the final UK tour of the year, with Franz supported by the Beat Up and Bob Long III. After shows in Ireland, Franz played three concerts at the Barrowland Ballroom, one of Glasgow's best-loved venues. One of the shows was a matinee for under-eighteens, during which Alex asked the audience for help with the lyrics to a song written as the Scottish World Cup anthem. The band also managed another Glasgow evening, this time in London where they hosted a Château night at the Scala in King's Cross. The band enjoyed settling back and watching the Kills, Kaiser Chiefs and Uncle John and Whitelock.

The UK tour had sold out in days, and extra days had been added at Manchester and London, where the band finished up at the end of the month. From there, it was on to Europe, and then there were commitments in Japan and America before the year was out. They were getting near the end of their touring for the year, but fatigue and lack of time and space to relax were beginning to show in the band.

The giddiness of the beginning of the first half of the year was giving way to weariness, which started to leak out into the band member's relationships with each other. Any group of people contains potential areas of friction, especially when living and working with each other in the stressful environment of live performance almost every day for a year. The stresses within the band eventually showed themselves in fairly spectacular fashion after a show at the Zenith venue in Paris. A crowd of reporters and Domino execs gathering outside the band's changing room for a short Gold Disc award ceremony, began to hear strange noises from within the changing room. A row had flared up between Paul and Alex over – of all things – Paul's choice of a red-and-black striped sweater for the ceremony. When Nick intervened the row escalated from a skirmish into all-out war, and words, fists and anything that came to hand were hurled around the room. Outside, the assembled media horde hushed to listen to the yelling match going on behind the door. In surreal fashion, the band then fixed smiles, emerged from their room to receive their Gold Disc, and then went back in to continue their bust-up. In the immediate aftermath of the event, which managed to find its way into newspapers all over Europe, the band and its management skilfully played down rumours of the band breaking up, instead pointing to the inevitable stresses of such a relentless touring schedule. In July 2005, however, Nick revealed to the *NME* that it had been a genuinely bleak moment for him, and that he had indeed considered leaving the band: 'Is it worth it? If we get on each other's nerves that much?'. He put the incident in perspective by remembering that he and Alex had first met in a fight over a bottle of vodka. A certain degree of tension and perhaps even conflict is perhaps just part of Alex and Nick's relationship.

As the band took time to recover their composure and continue their European tour, the Rich Costey-recorded 'This Fffire' was released in Australia. The video that went with it was a classic Franz Ferdinand visual creation, full of Constructivist and Dadaist references, but also merging real footage with animation – the band themselves turned into crazy-looking automatons, Nick resplendent with a mechanical eye.

In many ways, November was a month too far for Franz Ferdinand. They still had Japan and the States to visit, and their energy levels were getting seriously depleted. It did not help that they were nominated for three MTV European Music Awards, only to be pipped at the post in all three categories, worst of all by Maroon 5 in Best New Act. (It was easier to get over being beaten by Muse in Best UK and Ireland Act and Best Alternative Act.)

Nick was given an unexpected boost to his confidence at the end of what had been a pretty grim month when he was voted the fifth coolest person in rock by the *NME*. More amused than flattered, Nick's contribution to the accompanying interview in the magazine resulted in the best Franz Ferdinand quote of all time ('I just think badgers are great'), thus proving that he, rather than Alex, should have been group spokesman all along.

Franz Ferdinand might have been running out of steam, but sales of the records had not. To cash in on the steady popularity of the album in the States, Sony repackaged it with an added disc of B-sides and launched it in time for the band's return in December. Meanwhile, Franz were in Japan for the second time that year for a four-show tour, and it was Bob's turn to show the strain.

The first rumblings were on Friday night as the band travelled from Tokyo to Osaka, where they were due to play on Saturday. By the time of the concert, Bob was descending into full-blown gastroenteritis; he managed to make it through the show, albeit sitting down for much of it. The next night, Franz were due at Nagoya, but it was uncertain if they would play. Bob's sushi and fatigue-related illness had worsened and he had been whisked away to hospital in Osaka. Deprived of their bass player, the band were unsure if they should continue with their set. The audience held their breath, and prepared for the worst, but, an hour late, the three Franz members still standing appeared on stage. They proceeded to play an acoustic set for the first half of the show, and then called upon the services of support band the Beat Up's bass player Dino Gollnick to take Bob's place for some Franz crowd pleasers. With just a few hours' practice, Dino managed to pull it off, with the rest of the Beat Up joining Franz on stage for an encore of 'Michael'. As the rest of the band flew to the States for the next leg of the tour, Bob remained bed-bound for a few days before being well enough to join the tour. For the first few US shows, Bob's place was taken by Fiery Furnaces bassist Toshi Yano, who had played in support of the band enough to have picked up the bass lines.

A last burst of touring saw the band take on nine cities, including Mexico City,[20] in just eleven days. However, the end was now in sight, and Christmas must have seemed more than usually attractive to the band, as it brought with it the promise of relaxation and free time. Back in the UK, they enjoyed a refreshingly down-to-earth appearance at the tenth anniversary celebrations of the Guided Missile label. Appearing as 'A Touch Of Velvet' before an audience of between one and two hundred at Mildmay Social Club in Highbury, Franz Ferdinand were reunited with friends from Glasgow, including the Country Teasers and John McKeown (ex-Yummy Fur). The following night, Franz recorded a studio performance of 'Take Me Out' for a Christmas Day special of *Top Of The Pops*, and then were finally free to go home. Two sold-out homecoming shows awaited them at Glasgow's colossal Scottish Exhibition and Conference Centre, with support from a band from the early 1980s period that had influenced Franz, the Fire Engines, specially reformed for the occasion. With touring over, Franz could finally spend time with friends and family, and remember who they were and where they had come from. Alex also used the time to buy the Lanarkshire farmhouse that would serve as the band's new headquarters, complete with recording studio to work on the new album.

Franz Ferdinand had survived 2004, the year that saw them grow into a band of global stature. Not satisfied, they were already working on their second album, a work that would seal their hard-earned reputation and demonstrate that they were not content to rest on their laurels.

---

20. Where they appeared having politely declined an invitation to a Buckingham Palace reception.

12.
GLASGOW SOUL

By 1965, Scotland was awash with bands, most of which struggled to earn a living in the club and ballroom scene. Promoters such as the Universal Dance Agency, based in Glasgow, had over 200 bands to choose from. Only a tiny fraction of these made the transition to a major label, of which the Poets and Lulu and the Luvvers (the Luvvers were swiftly dumped) were the most prominent. Most of these were performing cover versions of chart hits and so failed to distinguish themselves from the horde. Others were more distinctive. It was at this point that the cream of Glasgow's bands began to emerge as something special. Rather than follow the watered-down pop route, these Glasgow groups, like the hero of Glasgow music Alex Harvey (who was at this point playing with a house band in the Dennistoun Palais, Glasgow) looked to the original source of the beat boom for their inspiration. They sought out hard-to-find songs from labels such as Stax and Motown. This interest in the 'genuine article' and wish to differentiate themselves from the mainstream sound led to the great tradition of Northern Soul. Again, many of the post-industrial cities of the north could identify completely with the situation of artists working out of Detroit and Chicago, cities that were both undergoing a process of change.

One of the first such soul-inspired groups was the Blues Council. Sometimes cited as the perfect Mod band, the Council consisted of Leslie Harvey (Alex's younger brother), Bill Patrick (ex-Soul band), Fraser Calder and James Giffen. Having built up a following at the Scene Club in West Nile Street, the Blues Council were signed to EMI and recorded the single 'Baby Don't Look Now'. However, on 12 March 1965, before the single could be released, they were involved in a terrible traffic accident in their tour van outside Edinburgh. Fraser and Giffen were killed. Although the single was released, the rest of the group disbanded, shattered by the loss of their friends.

While Edinburgh bands were getting more mainstream in their tastes and were content to churn out UK chart covers, Glasgow powered itself with the raw fuel of R&B and soul. Three bands in particular represent the pinnacle of the music scene in Glasgow in the mid- to late 1960s, three bands that would assert Glasgow's sub-cultural dominance over Edinburgh – a position it has yet to yield. They were the Gaylords (later to become the Marmalade), the Beatstalkers and the Pathfinders.

The Gaylords had started life as Dean Ford and the Gaylords on the standard ballroom circuit in the early 1960s. Their big break came in 1964 when journalist Gordon Reed succeeded in persuading EMI to come to Glasgow and check out the new talent. A two-day audition was held at the Locarno on Sauchiehall Street with producer Norrie Paramour in the judge's chair. EMI were looking for a group to set against Decca's now hugely successful Lulu. The Gaylords shone above the other competitors and were duly signed to Columbia. Their first single, a cover of Chubby Checker's 'Twenty Miles', revealed their growing interest in R&B, but despite selling well in Scotland, it failed to break into the national charts. Over the next couple of years, the Gaylords released two more singles with little impact. Deciding that they could better drive their career from London, the band moved south and, in 1966, released a single directly targeted at the Mod movement, 'He's A Good Face (But He's Down And Out)' – a face being code for a top Mod. Sadly, they had missed the boat, and the single once again failed to make a mark. Realising that they had tried everything, the Gaylords decided to undergo a major shift. They renamed themselves the Marmalade, transferred from EMI to CBS, and started all over again. This second incarnation proved more timely and more mainstream, with its swerve towards psychedelia and Beatles covers.

The Beatstalkers made their mark by hunting down exotic R&B imports and performing to likeminded audiences. Perfectly turned out in Mod style, this band also managed to keep their individual identities, rather than looking like the clone arrangements from earlier in the decade. They were seen as the hippest things in Glasgow, even earning the nickname 'the Scottish Beatles', and had a huge local following. If any proof of the fervour of their fans were needed, the events of 11 June 1965 provided it. Booked to play an outdoor concert in the centre of Glasgow, the Beatstalkers were delighted and slightly perturbed to find thousands of fans filling George Square. As the band took to the stage, the fans (numbering anywhere from five to eight thousand depending on the source) surged forward, in the process inflicting terminal damage to the temporary stage the Beatstalkers were perched upon. Mounted police had to make their way through the throng and rescue the band before the stage collapsed. The following day, the Beatstalkers were all over the papers and the near disaster turned into a publicity triumph. Signed to Decca, the band now faced the same challenge as so many other Glasgow bands, trying to translate local acclaim into national success. Their first single for Decca, 'Everybody's Talking 'Bout My Baby', was written for them by songwriter Tony Washington and sold 50,000 copies in the first month after its release in August 1965. However, most of the sales were in Scotland and so did not register in the English music charts. The label was baffled by this phenomenon of increasing popularity in Scotland and invisibility in England. Two singles followed in 1966 before the group switched to CBS later that year. The move brought the band under the management of Kenneth Pitt, David Bowie's then manager. After their debut for CBS also failed to find favour, Pitt started to nudge the band towards the psychedelic end of the musical spectrum. Unlike the Marmalade, however, the Beatstalkers never seemed comfortable in this territory. Their first single in this new vein was 'Silver Treetop School For Boys', a Bowie leftover that, due to its strongly autobiographical details, just seemed odd when sung by the Beatstalkers. More Bowie numbers followed, and the Beatstalkers just seemed to be getting lost in a swirl of psychedelia and Bowie's powerful imagination. Their manager was more focussed on the career of his star performer, and the Beatstalkers, like the Poets before them, were allowed to drift without proper guidance. In 1969, the band were already on their last legs when their van and equipment were stolen in Coventry. The Beatstalkers called it a day.

The Pathfinders, who started life as the Sabres in the early 1960s, like the Gaylords and the Beatstalkers, had their best period early on in their career, when they were cranking out gritty soul numbers to an appreciative Glasgow audience, usually at their favoured venue, the Picasso. Hungry for wider success, the band accepted an invitation from their friend George Gallagher of the Poets to go to London and seek out a record deal. The trip resulted in a meeting with ex-Shadows drummer Tony Meehan, then working as a producer. He liked the Pathfinders and agreed to take them under his wing, prompting their permanent move south in 1966. Meehan managed to get the band taken on by Apple, the Beatles-owned enterprise with a house record label. Immediately, the band came under the malign influences abiding in and around the already crumbling Beatles empire. The name Pathfinders was judged passé, and the extremely dodgy White Trash supplied instead – whether as a joke that was accidentally taken seriously remains unclear. Under this title the band recorded their first Apple single, 'Road To Nowhere' – the Carole King and Gerry Goffin number. Listened to today, the recording seems to promise much, but at the time it failed to make an impact. The situation was not helped by the last-minute reprinting required when it became clear that both the BBC and American broadcasters were unlikely to play the track if the name White Trash remained. Re-renamed Trash, the band struggled on. With increasing in-fighting between the company directors (the Beatles) going on around them, Trash saw the prospect of recording an album was receding fast. Bass player Colin Morrison got fed up and left; the others stuck around to see if things might get better. They didn't. The final Trash-Apple venture was the bizarre recording of the Beatles' 'Golden Slumbers' and 'Carry That Weight' as a double A-side with self-penned 'Trash Can' on the reverse. According to accounts from within the rotting Apple, it was Derek Taylor, the Apple Press Officer, who felt sympathy for Trash's position and so retrieved the acetates of the newly recorded songs for them to record without the Beatles permission. When they discovered what had happened, Paul McCartney said they couldn't release the single, but John Lennon said go ahead. They went ahead, reached Number 35 and returned north.

All three bands provided an important legacy for future Glasgow musicians, not only for what they did right, but for what they did wrong. Over the coming decades, Glasgow bands would grow ever more realistic and streetwise about how they could make an impact without throwing themselves completely on the mercy of major, London-based labels. As the 1960s ended, however, it seemed an era had passed and it wasn't clear where the next pioneer of Glasgow music would come from. But there was someone waiting in the wings, someone who had been there all along and who was just waiting for another chance: Alex Harvey.

13.
GLASGOW VOICES:
ROBERT JOHNSTON

A musician, artist and graphic designer, Robert Johnston was the guitarist in seminal Glasgow band Life Without Buildings from 1999 to 2002. The band's brief lifespan belies their importance: their one album, *Any Other City*, has become a true underground classic. Largely ignored at the time, it continues to win diehard fans five years after it was made.

There seems to be a strong connection between the art and music scenes in Glasgow. For example, you were all artists in Life Without Buildings, weren't you?

Sort of. I'd kind of finished with being an artist by that point. I don't really know how long there's been much of a strong connection. I think maybe partly it's just because the whole community in Glasgow is quite small and so there's a crossover between everything, not just between art and music. It tended to be that people who were interested in anything creative would be interested in all things creative, so you'd find that artists would tend to come to places where there is music played and they just sort of associate with musicians – because there are so many in Glasgow anyway. Per capita there are so many bands. I was always specifically a real music fan well before I was remotely interested in art, so when I drifted into the art scene I was lucky in a way, particularly when I was working at Transmission [a Glasgow art gallery] between 1997 and 1999, myself and another guy on the committee there, a guy called Ewan Imrie, we were both keen music fans and sort of wondered why there wasn't more of a real, genuine cross-over between the two scenes in Glasgow. We actually tried to implement that in a way. The 13TH Note [a café and arts venue] had just moved onto King Street, basically right next door to Transmission, so we did a two-week project: art projects went on in the 13TH Note gig space and bands played in the gallery, which had happened well before that in Glasgow, even five years earlier there was old Guitar Amp Action, which I think Ross Sinclair – an artist who was the drummer in the Soup Dragons – was involved with, so there's always been some sort of cross-over and it just sort of waxes and wanes over the years. I think it's really, really strong at the moment: all the main bands that are coming out of Glasgow have some sort of art connection, like Park Attack: Rob Churm was in the same year as Bob with Franz.

Did you train at the Art School?
Yeah, as a fine artist. I never really studied design or music. The Art School, Transmission and the 13TH Note form a triangle for a community of creative people. That's basically the way that things have worked: those institutions enclosing a fairly tight community, who do a lot of different things, not just music, but writing and design and all sorts of stuff.

Was that something you were conscious of with Life Without Buildings: a form of music that was on the artistic side of things?
I think we were really conscious of trying to resist that. There was a phenomenon around the turn of the twenty-first century when a lot of artists had bands. Things like Owada, Martin Creed's band, and Big Bottom, Angela Bulloch's band, and they were all kind of semi-joke bands that had this high concept behind them. The band was basically formed by myself and a guy called Will Bradley, and we were just huge music fans and had no patience whatsoever with the art-band nonsense. We wanted to just be a band, a group of musicians, and we were quite reluctant to do things like gigs in galleries, but ultimately when you get offered these sort of things and you need the practice, you just do them. It was never really any intention of specifically being arty. But certainly with someone like Sue, the singer, who obviously never had any real ambition to be a singer: she was an artist, that was the background that she came from and that was what she brought to the band. In the same way that someone like Patti Smith wasn't a singer in the conventional sense, or Mark E Smith. So that's sort of accidental, and part of a broad-minded approach to music rather than an artistic approach.

So was Sue's vocal technique a style of performance art that she had developed?
Yeah. She'd been doing them for years, initially written but then mostly

experienced as a performance, as a spoken-word thing: they were just really musical. Myself and Will and the bassist in the band, Chris Evans, had been playing together for a while and really were just absolutely hopeless – it sounded terrible. We got offered this gig and we decided that the only thing that was going to save us was if we got a really charismatic singer. Will knew Sue really quite well and as it happened Will happened to be at a show in Transmission where Sue did a performance along with her sister and a group of artists that included Victoria Morton, Cathy Wilkes and Sarah Tripp. Basically, we were just all standing watching Sue give this very magnetic, charismatic performance and it just struck us: why don't we ask her? We didn't really know if she could sing, because there wasn't really anything melodic involved in what she was doing at that time. It turned out that she could, which was a blessing, but we just asked her to do something with the band – and it was immediately apparent that it was going to work.

Life Without Buildings seemed to be a band that really connected with people, but were you successful within the UK?
No, not at all. I think, brass tacks, we sold about 2000 records, which is absolutely nothing. I think the people who liked us tended to really, really like us, and pretty much everybody else just ignored us. Some people really hated us, which I think is natural: what Sue was doing was quite abrasive to a lot of people's ears, quite difficult to take. To us and to those who got it, it was wonderful. We did well in Australia, weirdly enough, I don't really know why, and we did better in particular countries in the continent than we did in the UK.

Do you think Glasgow has a strong image to outsiders?
Yeah. Particularly through having grown out of the 1990s. People underestimate the size of bands like Mogwai and Arab Strap and Belle and Sebastian, I mean they're really huge abroad, in Japan, Australia and continental Europe, these bands are massive. I think the fact that they come from Glasgow is really well known, Glasgow's almost a sort of mythical city to a lot of kids that live in these places. Here in the UK, I think it's taken for granted to a certain extent, and it's also a lot harder for smaller bands to do well in the UK and to be visible. I think Glasgow is in a way a selling point for a lot of bands.

Skinny ties and sharp suits. Franz Ferdinand at the
47th Grammy Awards, Los Angeles, 13 February 2005

Top left: Barfly

Top right: Glasgow School of Art, Vic Bar and main entrance

Left: Stereo

Below: Bridgeton CID: jail, office and court complex

Top: Abandoned theatre

Above left: The Glasgow Grand Ole Opry lights up at night

Above right: Flourish Studios and the Modern Institute

Left: The Château

Benchmark Franz Ferdinand performance
on *Later With Jools Holland*, 3 November 2003

HMV, Oxford Circus, London, 9 February 2004

Victorious at the *NME* Awards, Hammersmith Palais, 12 February 2004

Clockwise from top left: Tramway, 13th Note,
King Tut's Wah Wah Hut and Sub Club

The band appear again on *Later With Jools Holland*, December 2004

Alex, Virgin Megastore,
New York, 15 June 2004

*The music and art scene is obviously close-knit, but is it co-operative or
competitive?*

I think it's a bit of both, but definitely more cooperative than competitive. I don't really know what it is particularly about Glasgow – one of the main factors is the absence of any sort of commerce in those areas. Up until recently, there really were no galleries selling contemporary art, there still aren't really any big record companies present here, there's a few good small ones, but the majors aren't here at all, and the A&R people don't come up really. So everyone's sort in the same boat of amateurishness – in the true sense of the word: people do it because they enjoy it and want to, and they do it in a way to participate and contribute to a community of people, rather than doing it for careerist reasons. It tends to be that when people decide they want a career, they move to London, and everyone who doesn't really want a career stays in Glasgow. The cream rises to the top, or sinks to the bottom, depending on which way you look at it.

*People in the art scene seem to be having some success at building
another level beyond the grassroots, so that local artists can have
international career from Glasgow. Does the music scene need to attempt
the same thing?*

Yeah, but it's so much harder in the music scene. I guess things are transitional at the moment, but certainly up until now the cost of producing vinyl or CDs, promoting bands, advertising and sending them on tour is huge and prohibitive. Things have really changed in the art scene over the past ten years where it's now possible to stay in Glasgow and have a really strong career, because the links between Glasgow and continental Europe are really strong and effectively you can bypass London completely; you don't need to go there to be a successful artist anymore, you can actually stay in Glasgow and have the support you need. You won't sell any work to anyone in Glasgow, but you can sell work from Glasgow to that international audience. In terms of record labels and bands, nothing's really changed that much. If you want to be successful quickly, I think you still need to go to London as a band or a musician. That may change with the advent of MP3 and the kind of technologies that may obviate the need for expensive manufacturing processes and things like that.

Are you doing more graphic design than music at the moment?
Well, it's a full-time job basically, it was even when I was in Life Without Buildings, but I took a lot of time out for the band. I quit Pro Forma about two months ago and just kind of accept the fact that really music's a hobby for me. I sort of came to the point when I realised that I didn't really want a career in music, I've got everything out of it that I wanted to get. I'm lucky enough to be good friends with some people who've done well and have careers in music, and I don't really like their lifestyles very much. The travelling, the promotion, the compromise you have to undergo, all these kind of things. It's a very high-powered, very pressured thing, and difficult to do. I mean, I think it's easy enough to do when you're 22, to be travelling constantly and to be drinking a lot and you know, etc., etc., but when you get to 32, it's not so much fun anymore, you just want a bit of an easier life. It's just not for me.

That's obviously sad for people who wonder where the elements of LWB will resurface musically. You are doing this little bit of work with Desert Hearts.
Yeah, I mean there's never going to be a point in my life where I'm not involved with music – most of my good friends are really heavily involved with it. It's always going to be a really big part of what I do. What I would like to think is that at some point the influence of Life Without Buildings might show. I think there's been some mild, vague influence surfacing recently.

Where do you see that?
I think in a way we were, by pure chance, a little bit ahead of our time, and I think if we'd popped up around the time of bands like Bloc Party and even Franz, we'd have looked a lot more part of things than we did when we did appear. Things might have been a lot easier for us, it would have been easier for a pop audience to understand what we were doing. Because we were *pop* music, I don't think we were avant-garde music – we were making pop songs. There are certain people in certain bands around at the moment who are really big fans of Life Without Buildings, and in a way I hope, because I'm very proud of the record that we made, at some point it might be seen in the way that maybe I see things like the Young Marble Giants' album: not many people know about it, but people who do know about it really love it and it means a lot to them and

it's influenced a lot of bands. It's quite submerged, but it's there. Maybe that will happen, but it is difficult to say.

Would the presence of a major record company be a good or bad thing for Glasgow?

It's almost pointless to speculate about that because a big record company would never crop up in Glasgow. Glasgow's definitely a very individual place but it's not unique: over the years there have been these real hotbeds, places like Manchester and Liverpool. I can't really remember the last time there was a really important musical movement that came out of London, even punk. I mean punk broadly didn't come out of London – the Sex Pistols did, but the movement was really a regional movement and was mainly oriented in Manchester. I think music tends to come out of places where the record industry isn't: it's just something that happens. It's just down to individual bands and musicians as to how they want to play it. You could spend all your days playing small pubs in Glasgow and not really doing anything financially with the music you make, or you could go to London and become a big business, or you could do something sort of midway. A lot of bands do quite well with the midway thing, particularly if you get involved in touring abroad, because it's actually financially viable and worthwhile to tour on the Continent or somewhere like Australia or even the States in a way that it's not in the UK. In the UK, touring's seen as promotional and you expect to lose a lot of money doing it, but you can actually have a career and make money as a touring band, and that's what bands like Arab Strap, Mogwai, Belle and Sebastian do: all these people actually make money and do well touring for an international audience. You never make much money out of record sales, if you write songs you make some money out of publishing maybe, but you can actually make a living touring, without really having to be a popular monster.

Glasgow's creatives are very good at using alternative spaces.

Yeah, and that happens everywhere. I wish it would happen more in Glasgow, actually. I went to Berlin a few years ago and there were massive opportunities over there with the opening up of the East. There are so many incredible spaces that people just take on and use over long terms, and basically just occupy and they become big institutions, like

Cookies, a really famous club over there, owns a massive space and has become a commercial concern. It started out as basically a squat. It doesn't really happen anymore in the UK, the squat scene is really pretty much dead now, and it never really existed anyway in Glasgow. That kind of taking over of alternative spaces is just something that's been done for years and years, particularly by artists, not so much by musicians. One of the interesting things that came out of the whole Franz art thing was the Château, and their involvement in that. That was really the first time that a band has taken advantage of art-world guerrilla building-adoption tactics, and it worked incredibly well for them – it's one of those gigs that's going to go down in history, I think it was quite instrumental in making their career. I don't think a band, to my knowledge, have really done that before, certainly not before the early 1980s anyway.

There was some recent controversy about the use of one Glasgow's most interesting spaces, the Tramway.
In a nutshell, the City Council wanted to sell off the space to Scottish Ballet. Art in Glasgow has never really been that well supported by local government, they don't really understand it and they don't like it very much. GOMA [Gallery of Modern Art] is a perfect example: when that started out it was basically a national laughing stock, actually an international laughing stock. It was headed up by a guy called Julian Spalding, who insisted that Glaswegians were too stupid to understand avant-garde, contemporary art – he didn't say that in so many words, but that's basically what he meant. He had this phrase: 'Art for the people', which meant a lot of Beryl Cook paintings and things like that. We had probably the most active group of contemporary artists maybe in any city in the world at that time, and we had a gallery of modern art that wasn't even aware they existed. It's changed considerably since then, but the situation still exists where the City Council is pretty ignorant of what's going on in terms of the art scene here. I guess most city councils are quite ignorant of contemporary art, but people actually come to Glasgow and bring money into the economy because of the art scene. The City Council hasn't even slightly tried to exploit that and it's baffling, because it could actually be a huge source of revenue to them. The Tramway thing really was just another example of that, and one of the bigger examples. It didn't come out of nowhere, it came out of a long

history of ignorance on the part of the City Council and it was basically the straw that broke the camel's back for many people.

Is the CCA [Centre for Contemporary Arts] any better?
Not really. The CCA started out as a place called the Third Eye Centre, which was actually really good and very, very radical, really prepared to kick up a fuss and show some quite difficult things. It gradually morphed into the CCA, which is really more of a safe, municipal art centre, it's valuable to a certain extent. It underwent a massive renovation, which was financed by I think seven million pounds of National Lottery money, the main upshot of which was that they turned most of it into a café. Which is again absolutely typical. I wouldn't want to play down the fact that there are actually good people working at the CCA, who, in difficult circumstances, do some quite good things. It's just it's not an ideal space and it's not the answer to anything.

You're due to do a session with Desert Hearts at Chem19 in a couple of days. Will that involve you doing your track and then heading off?
No, generally when those guys are in the studio and I get the chance I just like to go along. I've always had quite a good ear for recording. I've had a bit of experience, I know the terminology and the technology that's involved, so I tend to go along and sit on the couch and make comments. Maybe sometimes I'll put a little guitar overdub on something, but it's a tangential involvement, it's not like I go along and do a session, it's really just hanging out more than anything else.

Is Chem19 the main recording studio for Glasgow?
Until recently, there was a place called Ca Va. It was quite expensive and known for quite a clean sound: it's where Deacon Blue and bands like that recorded. I think for bands like us, in our position, we'd never worked with a recoding engineer before, we'd never been in a studio when we recorded part of our stuff and we'd heard all sorts of horror stories about engineers who weren't really interested in bands and would generally just sit there with their feet up on the console not doing anything except making sly comments. We kind of got the impression that Ca Va would be like that. Chem19 was just a bit cheaper, a bit friendlier and has Andy Miller, who's basically an absolute gem. He just

absolutely adores music. The thing about Andy is that he works incredibly hard to get performances out of people. That's really what he's interested in: hearing something happening and trying to capture it. He's in it for exactly the right reasons, he's incredibly overworked, as anyone who knows what they're doing generally is, and because he can't say no to anything. He works like 70-hour weeks and the most lunatic hours, and he contributes an immense amount I think to music in the city, just by his enthusiasm, by his willingness to do stuff, generally for less money than he should be doing it for.

He's got his own label going now – Gargleblast. If you were going to record anything, would that be where you'd choose to go?
Yeah. If... if! ... Life Without Buildings ever got back together, I think it would definitely be a Gargleblast thing. We actually talked for a little while about getting back together to play at the Gargleblast launch, but it never really happened.

When was the last LWB performance?
We played one song at the Polish Club, which is just near Kelvingrove Park. I can't remember what the occasion was, it was some party or other, possibly somebody's birthday. Basically Natasha Noramly [of Fuck-Off Machete] noticed that all four of us were in the room, which is quite unusual because Chris now lives in Amsterdam, and Will doesn't come out a lot. She went round to each of us individually and asked how we would feel about doing a Life Without Buildings song, and everybody kind of said yeah, thinking that everyone else would say no. So she went round everybody again and said well, everybody said yes so do you want me to go get my bass. So we did an impromptu version of New Town. It was very sweet. Before that, the last gig we played was at Stereo, which was maybe late 2002, early 2003.

What do you think the general outlook for Glasgow's art and music is?
It's going to be really interesting. The art scene's at a point of real transition at the moment. Some people disagree with me about this, but I think that it's now got to the point where the Modern Institute has become such a massive influence globally – they're effectively giving a lot of artists careers, they're one of the first stalls that all of the style

arbiters got to see at art fairs, people in the art world know about them and respect them very, very highly. As a result, kids are starting to move up to Glasgow to go to art school because the Modern Institute's here. Which is crazy in a way, it's a really strange thing to do. Glasgow's still a bit of a backwater – a lot of kids that move up here don't realise that. They think that when they move up here they'll immediately be granted a career if they make work that looks like Jim Lambie or whatever. I suppose that's a slightly cynical way to look at it, but I think that's a real sea change. As a result of that there's been a lot more attention paid by the press to what happens in the art scene. The City Council have been forced by that to pay more attention, very reluctantly, to the art scene. There are starting to be people living in Glasgow who are buying contemporary art, that's just a really radical change – it's very small at the moment, but I think that will gather momentum. In terms of the music, I really don't know, I think it just goes in waves, it's always been really strong, just in different ways, there are some really, really exciting bands around just now, but then there usually are. I don't think there are going to be any radical changes.

There hasn't been a Franz Ferdinand factor?
No, I don't think so, I really don't think so. I don't think people really feel that on the ground in Glasgow. I mean, it may be that there are kids exposed to a band like Franz Ferdinand more than they would be to other bands. But before Franz Ferdinand there was Travis, who were obviously a different kettle of fish coming from a much more trad point of view, but you know Franz Ferdinand are still a pop band, they write pop songs. They've been lumped in with the whole punk-funk thing, but that's not really what they sound like, they sound like Orange Juice most of the time. So there's a history to that and it's an ongoing thing. I don't think it's any sort of massive upheaval.

14.
ALL ROADS LEAD TO GLASGOW

Fact 1: Franz Ferdinand are a product of Glasgow. Fact 2: None of the four members are native to the city.

These two statements might seem contradictory, but in fact the story of the band's formation reveals that without Glasgow and its unique qualities, Franz Ferdinand would never have existed. This is even more the case because Nick, Paul, Alex and Bob were drawn to Glasgow from different corners of Britain and Europe. The central thread of the band's formation is the story of Alexander Paul Huntley Kapranos's journey to Glasgow and his meeting with Nicholas McCarthy.

Alex was born in Almondsbury, Gloucestershire in the south west of England. His father was a Greek academic who had moved to the UK to work and had married an English woman from Sunderland. The exact date of Alex's birth remains a matter of contention, as some sources quote 20 March 1972 as the happy day, whereas others have suggested he is about three younger than that birthday would suggest.

Alex was a bright child, and inherited the great Greek art of expounding subjects from his father. He also developed a strong taste for music at an early age, a taste that prompted his parents to buy him a fake red electric guitar – an instrument he used to play along with *Top of the Pops*. In the academic environment of his home, Alex was not content merely to follow music shows on TV and radio, but also started to compile a considerable record collection together with an encyclopaedic knowledge of popular music history. The other love of Alex's life was reading and writing. His natural creative gifts led to various teenage attempts at writing songs, an early start that ensured that by the time he was writing songs for performance in the Glasgow music scene his lyrical skills were considerably advanced.

As well as the usual media sources that fed children in the 1980s with their musical diet (through which he would develop a taste for Duran Duran and the B52s), the young Alex was also exposed to Hellenic musical traditions through his father, and through the family's annual summer holidays in Greece. Traces of Greek melodies, rhythms and cadences are audible in many of Franz Ferdinand's songs, from the opening chords of 'Jacqueline' to the staccato introduction to '40''.

Most of Alex's younger years were spent in his mother's native Sunderland (where he first adopted his mother's maiden name of Huntley to avoid the attention of local bigots), before the family moved to Edinburgh. It was here that Alex picked up the Scottish east coast drawl that is the most prominent characteristic of his speech, although it still overlays some northern English pronunciation. At 17, he gained a place on the University of Aberdeen's theology course, before moving on to the University of Strathclyde in Glasgow in the early to mid-1990s to study English and Computing. It was not just the esteem of the city's academic institutions that drew Alex to Glasgow, but also its reputation as a hotbed of musical activity.

Gradually, Alex immersed himself in the music scene, and soon got to know the key promoters, bands and venues in the city. Various odd jobs at venues around the city eventually took him to the 13TH Note arts café, where he took the position of promoter. It was here that Alex's musical education entered its most important phase. His job at the 13TH Note was to talent scout for new acts and decide which should play at the venue. He would also occasionally act as a promoter for one-off nights in other Glasgow venues, such as Nice 'N' Sleazy in Sauchiehall Street. His role as talent spotter and judge of musical prowess helped Alex develop his own ideas of what made a good pop act. It also taught him the ins and outs of the record industry as he watched bands struggle up the greasy pole of pop success, only to fall foul of any number of potential hazards along the way. His role as promoter was not an office-bound job, and Alex was also responsible for the layout of the venue and the sound system for gigs. He had to deal with bands (and their egos) on a daily basis, and saw first-hand the tensions and weaknesses that could break groups apart. Occasionally, he had to step in and take matters into his own hands when a group was behaving inappropriately in the venue. Stuart Braithwaite of Mogwai, whom Alex remembers as a teenage Goth, recalls the 13TH Note promoter 'punching out' a particularly troublesome member of a band called Cyanide Dolls. [21]

21. Cyanide Dolls drummer David Gow, who witnessed the event, subsequently moved on to Arab Strap and Sons And Daughters.

Alex's 13TH Note years brought him into the heart of the Glasgow music scene. During his tenure he helped to kick start the careers of some of Glasgow's most famous bands, including Belle and Sebastian, Bis, Mogwai and the Delgados, and gave hundreds of lesser acts a chance at success – on average, the 13TH Note puts on between three and six bands most nights of the week. The role also inspired Alex to continue with his efforts to further his own musical career. A music promoter is always a useful person to have in your band, especially if he can play keyboards, guitar, sing, and write songs. After some abortive solo efforts, Alex started his own group, the Blisters.

The Blisters' one album, which they released in 1997, after they had changed their name to the Karelia, is an important document in the story of Alex's musical development. The output of the Blisters/Karelia was almost all down to Alex, he wrote both the music and the lyrics. It shows him at an early, more extreme version of the foppish 'gentleman of pop' persona that he carried into Franz Ferdinand, but which he seems to be allowing to fade away as the band progress. The key influence for the Blisters was the late 1970s-formed London new wave band, the Monochrome Set. It was particularly through lead singer Bid's politely spoken but sometimes savage delivery that Alex found a way into his own vocal style. [22] Not blessed with a straightforward good singing voice, Alex instead took the Bid approach in aping the vocal style of the 1920s white jazz singers, who would croon their lyrics without breaking into the vulgarities of full-blown singing. As a result, the rest of the Blister's gradually followed suit into a strange 1920s, Mexican nether world – akin to a band you might find performing in a David Lynch dream sequence. The arch vocal delivery combined with Alex's highly barbed and cynical lyrics, most of which were about the 'vapid' nature of love, or took aim at a figure in society and launched a barrage of Mark E Smith-style satire, as in 'Post Feminist Business Woman' and 'Christian Chorus'.

The Blisters' first release came about thanks to Alex's position at the 13TH Note. As part of his duties, he had inherited the running of the legendary Kazoo Club night, which saw the launch of many of Glasgow's finest, including Belle And Sebastian and Urusei Yatsura.

22. By a twist of fate, Bid produced the Karelia's album.

The latter's inclusion on a Kazoo Club compilation in 1994 had brought them to the attention of the late great John Peel, who duly invited them to record a session for his Radio 1 show. With the proceeds, the band started their own label on which the first release was a joint single with the Blisters in 1995. Alex returned the favour by playing organ for the band on a subsequent recording. It was also the 13TH Note that enabled the Blisters to get three of the band's songs released on a 1995 Glasgow compilation. The year before, Douglas Sturrock, an A&R man with Cherry Red Records, had arrived in Glasgow to scout for local talent. [23] He went to an eight-band bill at Nice'N'Sleazy, which seemed a good place to start, and met the promoter who had put the evening together – which turned out to be a chap named Alex Huntley. Over the next year, Douglas returned to Glasgow on numerous occasions, staying at Alex's Dennistoun flat and being guided by him around the Glasgow scene. The result of Douglas's tour of Glasgow was the first of Cherry Red's esteemed 'city souvenir' series, consisting of recordings of local bands from British cities other than London. Then, as now, the music industry was extremely London-centric, and the city series played an important part in reminding the industry that music was being made in other parts of the land. Alex corralled the best up-and-coming bands on the Glasgow scene who had not yet been signed, and Douglas arranged for a recording session at Glasgow's Brill Building. As a gesture of thanks to Alex, Douglas included the Blisters in the line-up. The other bands were the Yummy Fur (with whom Alex played bass from 1998 to the band's demise in 1999), Trout, Pink Kross, and Lugworm, all of whom were distinguishable as part of a 'Glasgow sound', very much at the punk end of the spectrum. The band that stood out – and not in a good way – were the Blisters. When Jade Gordon of *Melody Maker* came to review the compilation, the Blisters were portrayed as an unwelcome interruption to an otherwise worthy collection of underground classics. To quote, 'By the end of the fourth track [of Trout], I'm slobbering over their garbled blues explosions, so the sudden changeover to The Blisters' particular blend of cocktail-geek is deeply resented. Thank God for the current goddesses of British underground punk, Pink Kross: horrible memories of The Blisters' pop-luck affectations are wiped out

23. Douglas now manages bands, including the up-and-coming Cherry Hinton.

bit by bit...' [24] Bruised but not bowed by this unfriendly reception, the Blisters eventually won a recording contract with German label Roadrunner Records, at which point they changed their name to the Karelia and recorded the album, *Divorce At High Noon*, released in 1997. The band shot a video for the second track on the album 'Love's A Cliché', in which Alex sports an impressive pair of sideburns and slicked-back hair, together with a suit and tie. The spirit of David Lynch is at work again as the band – with Glen Thomson on double bass, Allan Wylie on trumpet and Thom Falls on drums – appear on a small stage before a red velvet curtain in a dingy singles bar. Alex sings into a 1920s-style square microphone as he tells the audience how pathetic love is. Other highlights of the album include Alex's banjolele in 'Crazy Irritation' and bouzouki in 'The Infinite Duration'. After disappointing sales of the album, however, the Karelia wrapped it up.

After the failure of the Karelia, Alex entered a period of uncertainty. He played bass and rhythm guitar with the Yummy Fur, and then accepted an invitation to join the line-up of Edinburgh-based ska collective, the Amphetameanies. As it turned out, this was just the sort of upbeat and humorously self-derogatory band that Alex needed to blow out the detritus of his Karelia years – and to learn how to get an audience on its feet. The Amphetameanies continue to be purveyors of high-quality, upbeat ska laced with infectiously foot-tapping rhythms. The culmination of Alex's sojourn with the band was the 2000 album, *Right Line In Nylons*. On it, he is credited with 'clean rhythm and lead guitar, backing vocals, big drum and additional keyboards', as well as writing a number of songs. Despite their ska flavour, these songs, both lyrically and musically, prove to be a step in the Franz direction for Alex. 'Speed Fever' in particular, shows an innovative approach to lyrics – using truncated phrases to enhance both the rhythm and the theme, while album-opener 'Last Night' shows an interest in everyday – or everynight – goings on that he would carry on into the Franz lexicon in songs such as 'Michael' and 'Tell her Tonight'.

We leave Alex in early 2002, teaching English for Speakers of Other Languages and IT at the Anniesland College of adult education. Although still involved in the music scene, he is without a band and at

24. Jade Gordon, *Melody Maker*, 23 September 1995.

a point that might have seemed at the time like the end of his musical career.

It is arguable that without Paul Thomson and Bob Hardy, Franz Ferdinand might still have existed, but perhaps with a different sound. Without Nick McCarthy, however, the band could not have grown into its world-beating class. It was his fateful entrance into Alex's life that brought together the two essential creative elements of the band. Nicholas McCarthy was born in Blackpool, but moved with his family at a young age to Rosenheim, near Munich, in southern Germany, where his father had accepted a job with auto and aerospace corporation, Daimler-Benz (now Daimler-Chrysler). The benefits of an ex-pat existence included Nick's attendance at German-speaking schools and consequent fluency in German, as well as the superior German higher education options. Nick's parents took full advantage, enrolling their son at the Munich Conservatory, where he studied double bass and piano. There were also downsides to living an ex-pat existence, which include a hint of an identity crisis, the allure of the role of the outsider, and the background sense of 'not belonging'. Whatever the underlying reason, during the late 1980s and early 1990s, Nick fell in with a bad crowd in Munich and earned himself a reputation as a troublemaker, with favoured activities running from car theft to breaking and entering (the latter a talent that would come in handy when Franz were looking for venues). He also developed a slightly outré persona, wearing an assortment of hats and outlandish clothes. The temptation to exhibitionism must have been particularly strong in the ultra-conservative atmosphere of Munich, where the population traditionally do all their partying just twice a year, during the Fasching (carnival) of January/February and the Oktoberfest in the autumn. Just when things were beginning to look bleak for Nick's prospects, he found an outlet for his rebellion in music. Having left the Conservatory, he joined experimental jazz/world music ensemble Embryo, whose fusion of jazz, rock and African folk music opened Nick's eyes to wider horizons of musical adventure. One of three double bassists in the group, he toured with Embryo to Morocco and around Germany, and got to know many important figures in the European jazz scene.

With his ties to Munich now more or less broken, the world was Nick's oyster and he could have chosen anywhere as the location for his musical career. He chose Glasgow, which has a well-established and internationally recognised jazz tradition, as well as contemporary, experimental groups such as the Sun Ra Arkestra-esque Glasgow Improvisers Orchestra and the renowned, Domino-signed Bill Wells Octet. On arriving in Glasgow, Nick immediately immersed himself in this scene, playing in various outfits before finding his way into Scatter, an eight- or nine-person ensemble led by drummer Alexander Neilson. [25] Nick actually continued his commitment to Scatter long after he had joined Franz Ferdinand, playing double bass on their May 2003-recorded album *Surprising Sing Stupendous Love.*

The shortest journey to Glasgow was that of Paul Robert Thomson, although even he is not a local, having been brought up in Edinburgh. Born in 1976, he was artistic and musical from an early age, and as soon as he was old enough moved to Glasgow, where the music and art scene was more vibrant than Edinburgh's. He enrolled in a foundation course for Environmental Art (one of the most famous of the relatively new departments at the Glasgow School of Art), but the experience merely convinced him to concentrate on music. Although sometimes dismissed in the press as simply the cheeky Glaswegian drummer of the group, Paul is proficient on a number of instruments, including keyboards, guitar and vocals, as well as doing a fine line in DJ-ing.

The first notable band with which Paul played in Glasgow was the Yummy Fur. [26] By this time (1997), the Yummy Fur had been around in various configurations for five years, with new members revolving around the central figure of John McKeown. The best way to describe the Yummy Fur is: thoroughly depraved, but in an entertaining way. Rumours abound of an infamous video the band recorded in which innovative uses were made of tampons, but copies of this mid-1990s gem have now gone (probably literally) underground. Musically, they sounded like the Velvet Underground would have sounded had they been formed in Glasgow in the 1990s, if such a thing can be imagined. Lyrics frequently broached touchy subjects, often sex but also anti-religious

---

25. Neilson accompanied the enigmatic Texan musician Jandek in a rare live performance in Glasgow in October 2004.

26. The band were named after a comic by Canadian cartoonist Chester Brown. The blackly humorous, surreal comic included the adventures of Ed the Happy Clown, who has the top of his penis replaced by Ronald Regan's head.

themes – always guaranteed to cause a stir in Glasgow. Paul's drumming can be heard on their last two albums, *Male Shadow At Three O'Clock* (1997) and *Sexy World* (1998), and is very much as demanded by McKeown – Mo Tucker-style smashing and steady rock rhythms rather than the funk-disco riffs he would develop for Franz Ferdinand.

As with most members of the Glasgow, or indeed any, music scene, Paul had to find ways to supplement his income. One of the ways he did this was a long stint as a model for life-drawing classes at the Glasgow School of Art. In the process, he was drawn by Fine Art students, who included future Franz bassist Bob Hardy and future friends and girlfriends of Franz Ferdinand members. Other routes to ready cash included being a hospital porter, a call centre telephonist, a laundry worker and even at one time selling grafts of tissue from his buttocks for medical research. He later complained that he thought he was getting £250 for each slice, whereas it turned out to be an all-in price.

Paul's next band gave him a chance to open his creative wings. Pro Forma formed in 2000 around Simon Henderson, a musician and promoter with a wealth of experience of the Glasgow scene. Together with Paul and Simon's sister Victoria, the group headed out into what was then new fairly new territory for Glasgow. The 1990s had seen Glasgow become a bastion of guitar bands, from the punky fringe captured on Cherry Red's compilation to the post-rock splendour of Mogwai and Ganger to the nascent nu-metal scene. Guitars continue to be the weapon of choice for most Glasgow bands (especially because the scene is so focused on live performance), but by the end of the 1990s the wider resurgence of electronica was making an impact locally. Simon, Vic and Paul were interested in exploring this branch of pop, and set to work on creating some of the finest tracks to come out of Glasgow at the time. With references to Joy Division and the Fall, with a dash of techno and generous drizzle of Suicide, Pro Forma managed a skilful blend of analogue and digital sounds to create a brave new universe in sound. [27] The band were also influenced by their contact with the Glasgow art scene, with which the music scene frequently merged. Pro Forma's forward-looking music took to the same wavelength as many of the artists working in Glasgow at the time, and some of their first releases were on

27. Pro Forma described their music as 'council house'.

compilations by record label Shadazz, which concentrated on showcasing music and art crossovers. The results of the crossover for Pro Forma included a video by Glasgow-based artist Torsten Lauschmann, and a sleeve design by artist and musician Lucy McKenzie.

Paul and Simon shared the responsibility for most of the instrumentation, programming and vocals, while Vic played bass and vocals. This early incarnation of Pro Forma issued their first release through the OSCARR (standing for Optimo Singles Club and Related Recordings), the label started by the organisers (Keith McIvor and Jonnie Wilkes) of the famous Optimo and Espacio club nights at Jamaica Street's Sub Club. Every month, the Optimo night features a live performance, of which Pro Forma were a strong favourite. The release was a four-track 12 inch, featuring 'Human Error', 'The Passion Prefix', 'Sexual Design' and 'Cracked Machine'. This EP featured the Lucy McKenzie sleeve, but sadly the distributor went bust before all the copies could be shifted. The four tracks were subsequently included – along with 'Ist Schön' and 'The Passion Prefix' video – on CD through the London-based Tsk! Tsk! label in 2004, no doubt partly thanks to Paul's by then considerable fame as the drummer of Franz Ferdinand. Paul left Pro Forma to join Franz Ferdinand in 2002, but the Henderson siblings have carried the torch and the band is still a welcome feature of the Glasgow scene today. Paul's place was filled by Will Bradley on drums and Robert Johnston on guitar and programming. Both were fresh from their experiences in another of Glasgow's most influential and underrated bands, Life Without Buildings, and both were heavily involved in the Glasgow art scene. Today's line-up includes Simon and Vic, Colin Kearney (ex-Eska) on drums and keyboards and Chris Leo on guitar.

The final piece of the Franz Ferdinand jigsaw, the poetically named Robert Byron Hardy, took perhaps the most conventional route to Glasgow, and one that had nothing to do with music. Born in 1980 and brought up in Bradford, Bob showed an artistic flair and gained a place on Bradford College's BTec foundation course in art and design in 1998. The standard of his work was high enough for him then to be accepted into the prestigious Glasgow School of Art Fine Art department, where he completed his first year in 2000. Remembered by his fellow students for his sense of humour and openness about his work, Bob was a popular figure and attracted a large group of friends around him. Keen to sample all that Glasgow had to offer, Bob became a regular at the various venues where artists and musicians gather to drink, chat and dance. One of these was the 13TH Note, which was situated on King Street, just a few doors down from one of Glasgow's most renowned art galleries, Transmission. Although reportedly at first put off by Bob's politically incorrect humour, Alex became firm friends with him, despite an age difference of between five and eight years (depending on which of Alex's birth dates you go with). Just as Bob was an artist interested in the music world, Alex was a musician with a growing interest in the art world. Bob's friends on the Fine Art course also proved interesting company for Alex, and through them he honed his art knowledge and developed a particular taste for the work of the Dadaists and Russian Constructivists, which were both popular influences among students at the time. This group of art school friends would prove an important part of Franz Ferdinand's final incubation, during which the ideas that would go into the formation of the band were thrashed out over pints and cigarettes. Both Alex and Nick would subsequently go out with members of Bob's year, and some of their important early shows would come about as a result of their art world contacts. This was just one crucial ingredient that Bob brought to the band, along with his relentless, northern sense of humour and warmth.

Although fatefully lured by Alex into the music world with the offer of a bass and guitar lessons in 2002, Bob carried through his commitments at the art school and graduated in 2003 with a BA (hons) in Fine Art (Drawing and Painting). For his degree show, he cheekily wrote to writer Will Self and David Bowie to ask them to contribute. He included a PS to Bowie that if he was busy, perhaps he could pass the request on to Brian Eno. None of them replied. That Bob did indeed graduate is a miracle in itself.

The speed with which Franz Ferdinand rose to success was dizzying: Bob started learning the bass at the end of his third year at art school, and by the end of his fourth (his graduation year) Franz were a major act with a hectic gig schedule and contract with Domino. He follows a long line of Glasgow artists who have crossed over into music (Lucy McKenzie, Will Bradley, Robert Johnston, Paul Thomson, Jonnie Wilkes, etc.), many of whom returned to art later on in their career. It remains to be seen whether Bob has turned his back on his art practice for good.

All four members of Franz Ferdinand were now in Glasgow, moving in more or less the same circles. All they had to do now was meet.

15.
GLASGOW VOICES:
NATASHA NORAMLY

C oming to Glasgow via Kuala Lumpur, Australia and Europe, following the United Nations career of her father around the world, Natasha Noramly's first band was Fukuyama, followed by the last incarnation of Ganger (she was one of the band's two bass players). After the demise of Ganger, she started her own band with Callan Dickson and Paul Mellon, naming the group Fuck-Off Machete and recording a debut album with funding from the Scottish Arts Council on the Lost Dog label. Natasha is also a founder member of simbiotic, a successful Glasgow-based Internet company.

I've just been listening to My First Machete *and really enjoying it.*
That was done when we were only three months old. It's very young Fuck-Off Machete. Basically, we had just advertised for our guitarist, and he had only just joined the band. We wrote everything in about three months and wrote a couple of songs in the studio. It's a really interesting record for me because the tracks were really new. I think they've developed a lot more live now, but it's really indicative of the time with the new band's line-up. There's a few songs on there that I really do think we captured and wouldn't have got any better, but a lot of our new songs are really different. But, you know, it was the best thing we could do at the time and I'm proud of it.

We worked with Andy Miller, who recorded the Sons and Daughters album, the Mogwai singles that were single of the week in the *NME*, early Arab Strap. He works for Chem19, Chemikal Underground's recording studio. He's a really incredible producer.

So he had a strong input to the sound?
Oh, absolutely. The way he works is he's more like a friend. It's all about feeling really comfortable with him and he's just really encouraging. When I wrote this, I hadn't learned to sing and play bass at the same

time. I'd hardly done any vocals before, because my previous band was instrumental – Ganger. So he was really integral in pushing me to do those things together. It's very difficult, especially because a lot of the vocals follow the guitar. So it's difficult to follow the guitar with the vocal, but play something different on the bass.

How did you come to team up with Lost Dog?
Lost Dog are quite a small label up here. They've just put out the El Hombre Trajeado album, and they have another band on their roster called Soyuz. Basically, we were funded by the Arts Council for the album, which is part of the reason it was done when we were only three months old because we were given the opportunity and we were like 'we've got to do this now'. The reason why we're looking for a new label is we need somebody to fund it. We were lucky with this one because the Arts Council funded it, but unfortunately Lost Dog don't have the funds to send us in the studio for four weeks.

I was at Optimo last night, where there was such a refreshing mixture of music: Johnny Cash fading into techno.
And Optimo's been busy for years. In fact, my band were the very first band to play live at Optimo, and that was seven years ago. I used to be in a band called Fukuyama: we had a couple of singles out. We did our set at Optimo behind the DJ booth with an acoustic guitar and a bass plugged into the mixing desk.

How did you fit?
We just crouched down, no one could see us, it was great.

How long have you been over here? Did you used to live in Australia?
Yeah. I was there for a little bit. I'm half Malaysian. I've been in Europe since I was eleven. My Dad had a job in Vienna. Do you know Hans Blix?

Yeah
He was my Dad's boss. He was a really nice guy actually. Eva and Hans. So we lived there, my Dad worked for the UN, and then we moved to Australia and then I moved to Glasgow.

And what was it that drew you to Glasgow?
I got accepted into Bristol, Edinburgh, Glasgow, London and Norwich. What I did was I got the *NME* and I just looked at where all the bands were going, and it was just like Glasgow, Glasgow, Glasgow, Glasgow. That's fine, I'll go there.

So when was that? 1996?
No, it was 1994. I'm older than I probably look.

I've said the right thing then. Who was around then? Bis, had they started?
Yeah. Stephen used to be the drummer for Ganger, actually. When Fukuyama were around, Mogwai, Arab Strap, Snow Patrol, and all of Alex's previous bands were around then. El Hombre Trajeado were around. So the post-rock thing was definitely happening back then.

Has the scene developed since then? Or do you look back on a period and think 'that was the best'?
I think 1996, around then, was a very strong year for Glasgow, when Mogwai were just emerging, that was really new and it was a really strong period. Mogwai and bands like that were definitely quite unusual in their sound. I think maybe as a genre, that's more identifiable than what's happening at the moment, which is a merging of garage rock and guitary-type music.

Franz Ferdinand are looking back to the late 1970s and early 1980s with a lot of their stuff. Is that an era that you're conscious of when you're writing?
Not at the moment. In fact, I don't think I have a lot of 1970s music at all. I was an 1980s girl.

What sort of things were you listening to then?
I've seen a-ha in concert, Michael Jackson, Duran Duran. And I went to see David Hasselhoff and Kit. That was definitely one of the highlights of my childhood. It was really good, because he turned into a werewolf halfway through.

How surreal. Is there anyone in the Glasgow scene that has particularly helped you along?

simbiotic. I'm involved in simbiotic, but actually I would say they're allow-ing a lot of bands to do things. Let's say when I was in Ganger, we would have been able to have a sale online and things like that. They represent about 100 bands and record labels online. I think Teenage Fanclub are releasing an online-only album with them. The way simbiotic works is that they spend a few years developing e-commerce or something like that, but instead of selling it to just one person, they share it amongst everybody for free so that everyone can use it, sharing code and things like that. So bands that don't have any money can sell things online: simbiotic take a small commission. They kind of tie themselves into the success of their clients. They do Belle and Sebastian, Tindersticks, Biffy Clyro, Mogwai. They have from really tiny artists to really big labels. They also work with the opera, so it's really broad. So they're actually allowing bands and record labels, especially now with the distribution problems, to get their records out and tap into niche markets. The internet's really good for niche mar-kets and allowing somebody in America to get a Machete record that they wouldn't be able to get normally, linking people that are interested.

The people within simbiotic, half of them are technical and half of them are creative and the creative people are telling the technical people what we actually need, as opposed to the technical people saying 'Oh, this sounds good, you should have this all-singing, all-dancing site.' The interesting thing about the Internet is that people in bands and record labels are more demanding on technology, they are asking for things that law firms and accounting firms are only asking for a few years later. You know, bands and record labels wanted to update their own websites years before anyone else thought about it. They were like, 'I'm on tour, why can't I update my own website? Why do I have to know HTML?' They were asking technical people to do that way before anyone else: contact management systems and things like that. It's actually really good for a technical company to be working within the creative indus-tries because it keeps them ahead of anyone else.

Franz Ferdinand are using their website a lot. They're even putting on photos of them every day doing things around the house...
And the fans love it. You know the Q and A in the Mogwai section is the busiest page of the whole site. Fans get to ask some questions and the band reply totally snidely and people love it, they just say 'More!'. It's

definitely a medium of having that distance between your fans but being able to really communicate with them.

Which are your favourite Glasgow venues, either to watch a band or play yourself?
Well, obvious ones like Sleazy's have always been good, Mono and Stereo, but recently there's been a lot more inventive venues popping up. Triptych seem to be really good at putting on shows in churches, and the debating chamber at Glasgow University is just an amazing venue; Low played there: it's all wooden, so the sound is really interesting, and it's in this big old stone building with big leather armchairs. Whenever we need to practise for a show, we run private Machete gigs called My Private Machete. Basically, we invite people into our rehearsal room or just into some little bar somewhere. It brings people into a really personal space with the band.

What background do your other two band members have?
Not any background, which is really good actually. Paul's really young, he was only 21 or something when I met him, and Callan's from a little town up in Stirlingshire called Alloa. He only listened to ragga and reggae and that's it. He wasn't interested in any guitar music. He hadn't heard of Mogwai, he hadn't heard of Sonic Youth, hadn't heard of Pavement. So it was really interesting, because the stuff that he brought was really uninfluenced by any guitar bands. And Paul, being a 21-year-old, hadn't been battered down by the music industry and was just naively happy about being in a band, so it was a really amazing combination. Ganger, although I learned a lot being in that band, was a very dark band. We definitely all had a love-hate relationship with each other. That's what made it work: we hated each other so much that we were able to create some really interesting music. At the same time we loved each other, but we really didn't get on. I never realized that being in a band could actually be fun. It was really stressful being in that band. We went on tour in America for two and a half months once and our driver had a haemorrhaging eyeball from stress from driving us. We had to take him to hospital. And our drummer had a stroke through stress.

Not a happy period, then?
No, but I didn't know anything different. I'd never been in a real, proper

band that went on tour and did gigs and things. Very dark times. We recorded *Hammock Style* under a slaughterhouse in Edinburgh. In winter. For three weeks. And we stayed there. No shower, no kitchen. And we slept there. 24 hours, darkness, no light, nothing around. And dogs.

It sounds like you were almost daring each other.
Yes: 'How bad can we make this?' And so I didn't even think that there could be an option of maybe staying in a hotel or commuting or anything. Underneath the slaughterhouse for three weeks. It was a very dark time, but you listen to the record and it's not that dark. I can hear stuff in it, but it's actually quite a happy record.

There seems to be both light and dark in My First Machete.
What I like in this record is the dichotomy between the edginess and the really beautiful chords. I'm aware of that and it's something that I like. It keeps me interested and I hope it keeps other people interested. You can't just accept everything, you need to question a few things, there's a little question mark behind meanings and feelings and I think it helps you reinterpret songs, so the tenth time you listen to this album you might see a different side to a song than when you first listened to it.

Do you gear your songs towards performance or recording?
I guess I feel sometimes in terms of recording and sometimes in terms of performance. We're just about to do another tour later this year and for a lot of shows in London we only get about half an hour. So we've actually changed a lot of the songs to gear it to performance. In fact, 'Sudosu' we've cut in half...

Oh no!
It's actually really good! Just so we can fit in more songs. The other reason we have to think about performance is that I use very strange tunings on my bass, and I use a capo, which I've never seen anyone else do. So a lot of our performance is governed by what I can play next. You have to have little interludes for me to be able to quickly change the capo. I can't afford another bass, but as soon as I do that our performance will probably change, because at the moment it's: this one has to come after this one.

You use the bass in a very unusual way.

I'm not trained, nobody taught me how to play bass, so I never really knew what the standard tuning was. Obviously, being in Ganger was quite experimental in terms of having two basses, you had to be creative with the way you used it and I used to capo it up to try and get different tones to the lower bass – it just kind of stuck with me. So, although it's very different from Ganger, there's a little bit that followed through into this record. The way I play bass is more like a guitar a lot of the time. Me and Paul use the same plectrum, really light, I do a lot of strumming and sometimes he does basslines on his guitar because he's like 'You're playing the guitar line!' It's also unusual that the bass wrote a lot of these songs. We all write out separate bits, but sometimes the melodies have come from the bass, the initial 'Hey, here's an idea', and I think for a band that's really different. I can't stand those really dum da dum dum bass lines, I couldn't play like that.

How do the lyrics fit into the composition?

I definitely focus more on the sound of words as opposed to the meaning. I might want that meaning, but if it doesn't sound right, I can't use it. I don't feel comfortable using it. I have so much respect for some bands who can use words that I wish I could use, but I just wouldn't be comfortable saying them. Pavement and people like that: I just think 'How did you fit that word or sentence in the song and make it sound good?' I am very specific about my words and sometimes if I have a few words I really like it will take the direction of the meaning – I'll write a scenario around those words. Certain songs on the album are specifically about something: 'Sanctuary' is about a place I visited in Australia once, that was a very specific story. A lot of the new material has quite hooky sentences, said in different ways. The first song we did probably only has four sentences in it.

You've also got a really interesting vocal technique, whispering where many others would be shouting.

When I was trying to explain to Andy [Miller] what I wanted when I first met him, I said I wanted the vocal to be really close, like you're listening to it in headphones all the time. That was one of the things about performance: I had to learn how to do the 'whisper-shout', because you've got the drums – they won't turn down – and I like to play loud, and it's how to project your voice in a really quiet way as loudly as possible.

I have to ask: where did the name come from?
In fact, the band was named by somebody else. But we just loved it. It's not a swear word because it's got a dash. It's an adjective. It's a big, fuck-off machete. I don't really look at that and see swear words, I think it's partly the font as well. But it was hard to tell my mum. People either really hate it or really love it. A lot of people are like 'You'd do so well if it wasn't for the name.' But you know, if people like it they'll work round it.

How did the cover image [a boy holding a machete aloft] come about?
I have this machete. It's hand-painted by a guy who buys his machetes from Brazil and paints them with really serene images of fish and turtles. The one I got has a turtle. He's in England somewhere, probably a total nutcase.

A machete artist.
Yeah, he paints beautiful serene sea-life images on these, like, weapons. I mean this machete has channels for blood to go down, it's such a weapon, you know, and it's got a turtle on it. I don't want to sound clichéd, but the music is a little bit like that. It's got that rawness and then this really turtle bit. I just really loved it. It's perfect. And this little kid is in a band called Bladderpatch, he's a little death-metal kid. I saw him at the studio and we just fell in love with him. I found out when their next gig was, went to this underage, nu-metal, crazy gig, and found him – stalked him. We just loved him because he's got these mad curls and he looks like Diego Maradona. He's only about 12 and we thought he's just perfect for the cover. We took him out for a photo shoot and got him to pose, and then realized that we hadn't asked his mum. Colin [Hardie] from the label had to go out and speak to the parents and say 'Look, we want to use your son for the cover of an album.' She's like: 'All right...'. 'We've already taken the pictures for it. She's like: 'Right...'. 'He's holding a machete.' 'Right... and what's the band called?' 'Fuck-Off Machete.' 'Right, so you've already taken my son – my 12-year-old son – out, you've given him a machete, and he's been posing for two guys we don't know?' 'Yeah. Can you sign this form?

16.

EXILES AND EXPERIMENTS

By the end of the 1960s, there was a general feeling that things had gone as far as they could. The iconoclastic youth movements that came to define the era had lost their momentum, shrouded in a haze of hash and LSD; the economic drive of the post-war years had begun to wane; and the freshness and exuberance of rock 'n' roll had become bogged down in the flabby excesses of psychedelia and prog rock. In under two decades, rock music had been born and reached an outer limit, its early exponents greedily rushing into new ground at every opportunity, soon to find that they had left the garden of rock altogether and plunged into the forest of... art music. Throughout this giddy rush of musical discovery, Glasgow had shown a taste for the simple, beautiful, direct essence at the heart of rock music. It had shown this taste with its love of black American music and by its constant returning to this core of rock. Bands such as the Poets, the Beatstalkers and the Pathfinders had set out, as their very names suggest, to seek something more than just pop. It was their very success in this search that led them down to London and the mainstream, where their music got lost in the general winding down of the Swinging Sixties.

One positive effect of 1960s psychedelia had been the reinvigoration of the Glasgow folk scene. In the mid-1960s, the folk scene, which centred on Clive's Incredible Folk Club on Sauchiehall Street and the Glasgow Folk Centre off George Street, was in full swing. Both the USA and Britain were undergoing a folk revival, but it was in Glasgow that something new and different happened. Influenced by psychedelia, a group of folk musicians began to expand their music into more than just protest songs and traditional ballads. They took the folk sound and applied it to a more mystical, more ideologically aware style that would prove hugely influential to a whole generation of both folk and rock musicians. Foremost among these pioneers were the Incredible String Band and John Martyn.

Outside the folk sub-culture, the search for the essence of rock music was taking Glasgow's musicians into heavy territory. Espousing the raucous end of the musical spectrum, bands such as Gully Foyle, Power of Music, Sleaze Band and Tear Gas took their cue from heavy-metal pioneers Led Zeppelin and Deep Purple. This seeking out of the gritty core of blues-based rock music was a reaction to the increasingly slushy middle ground of pop that the 1970s generated, a reaction in the tradition of the previous back-to-basics movements. These two polarities of popular music – the slushy and the gritty – were reflected in the musical product of Scotland's top two cities. While Glasgow continued to champion music that drew upon the original blues source of rock 'n' roll, Edinburgh's contribution could be summed up by the words Bay City Rollers (until 1976 anyway, and with obvious exceptions like the Boston Dexters). This reinforcing of the notion of Edinburgh as the purveyor of mainstream music with mass appeal and Glasgow as home of the subculture reaction to that mainstream was crucial to the development of the Glasgow scene's character. Again and again, it would be the sub-culture that produced the most vibrant and fertile artistic product, while the mainstream ossified and stagnated.

Waiting in the wings while the 1960s were petering out was Glasgow's patron saint of rock music, Alex Harvey. After his stint in the house band of the Dennistoun Palais in Glasgow – where he had been joined by his guitar-playing younger brother Les, Bill and Bobby Patrick, ex-Poet George Gallagher and singer Maggie Bell (subsequently replaced by Isabel Bond) – Alex had drifted down to London once again to try to re-launch his career. It was 1967 and the English capital was still were it was at, but Alex was remembered as a dinosaur from another age (all of four years earlier), if he was remembered at all. This was the nadir of Alex's career; he drifted into nine months without work. On the point of giving up for good, he happened to come across another patron saint of rock, a young American guitarist who was reinvigorating the music scene by reminding audiences of what was possible. Any self-respecting rock musician who was around at the time has a Jimi Hendrix story, but for Alex Harvey it was at a pivotal moment in his life. In the stale *fin de siècle* atmosphere of the late 1960s, Hendrix sounded to Alex like something new, but the same. 'After hearing Hendrix, I knew I couldn't pack it in. The next day I was offered a job in a night club.'[28]

28. Martin Kielty, *SAHB Story*, p. 11.

The club job was no triumphant return to fame and fortune, but it was at least paid musical work. By putting his face and sound about, he made connections and was eventually asked by Derek Wadsworth, the musical director of the hippy musical *Hair*, which was transferring to London from Broadway in late 1968, to work in the pit band for the show. Despite the tedium of such a repetitive output – performing the same songs every evening and twice on Saturdays – the three years Alex spent in the *Hair* band were probably the closest to normality and family bliss that he achieved in his life. The meagre but regular income lent stability to his life in the Highgate house he shared with second wife Trudy, young son Alex and baby Tyro. His brother Les and singer Maggie Bell were also frequent visitors on Sundays, the one free day of the week. In terms of his musical career, it was just the sort of structured, guided reintroduction to the world of music that he needed; he would later admit that, while he found the work boring at times, it taught him discipline, an element that, unlike drive, passion and energy, had been missing in his work up to that point.

Having learned how to make a life in music sustainable, he set out once again to launch his career. One of the benefits of working in *Hair* was that it was evening work only during the week, and so allowed him plenty of time to develop other projects. For the first of these, in 1969, he gathered a group of likeminded collaborators, including Les on guitar and Derek Wadsworth on trombone, to record the album *Roman Wall Blues*. He even had his obligatory brush with psychedelia when he briefly worked with Giant Moth, with whom he released two singles on Decca. However, the real start of Alex's second career was marked by the arrival of Bill Fehilly, the Glasgow bingo entrepreneur and music promoter who had helped his early career and now took Alex on via his fledgling management company, Mountain Managements. Three events had so far conspired to keep Alex Harvey playing music: his witnessing of the guitar miracle that was Jimi Hendrix, his sojourn with the *Hair* band, and the timely appearance of Bill Fehilly. One final event would be added to these, one that would either confirm Alex's renewed dedication to music or end it altogether.

While Alex was exiled on Shaftesbury Avenue, his brother Les had teamed up with Bill Patrick – friend of the family and veteran of the Soul Band years – and Maggie Bell to form Power. This band was one of the vanguard of Glasgow bands seeking out heavier territory in search of a way to counter the pincer movement created by the excesses of prog rock on one flank and the increasingly saccharine and anodyne mainstream pop on the other. It was a movement informed by Deep Purple and Led Zeppelin, but more so by the Glasgow tradition of solid blues and soul music. Formed in 1967 in the Burns Howff on West Regent Street, a venue that became a headquarters for many likeminded bands,[29] Power consisted of Les, Maggie and two regular performers at the Burns Howff, John McGinnis and Jimmy Dewar. They started off performing gutsy blues covers, which, topped by Maggie Bells powerful but beautiful voice, earned them a regular following.

A pivotal moment came when Les Harvey was offered a place in another Scottish band, Cartoone, for a tour of the States. It was not an opportunity to be missed, and Les spent two months on the tour, during which he got to play with the then up-and-coming Allman Brothers. Inspired by his experiences, Les returned to Power with the conviction that they should start writing their own material – and he already had some song ideas to start them off. The result was that Power turned from a pub band to an act that started making ripples in the wider music industry. Songwriter and producer Mark London who had put Les in touch with Cartoone, invited his friend Peter Grant to watch a Power gig in Glasgow in 1969. Grant was already moving into the upper echelons of the rock hierarchy as the manager of Led Zeppelin, who were fast becoming the biggest band on the planet, and turned up to the humble venue in a limo. Not daunted, Power put on a show that impressed Grant sufficiently for him to take the band on under his and Mark London's management. The cockney Grant's favourite expression, 'stone the crows', was adopted as the band's new name, and they moved to London to record their first album. In a situation reminiscent of the Poets' connection with the Rolling Stones and the Gaylords' with the Beatles, the band were accepted into the Led Zeppelin inner circle, with Les and Maggie even moving into the Swan Building at 484 Kings Road, home of Swan Song Records. Unlike their fellow Glaswegians, however, Stone The Crows enjoyed considerable success with their move south. The eponymous debut released in 1970 and subsequent classic

29. The traditional ballroom venues were in continuing decline.

Teenage Licks in 1971 put the band firmly on the map and won a Best Vocalist title for Maggie in the 1972 *Melody Maker* Readers' Poll.

The exciting prospects of the band were cut short in a particularly cruel and tragic fashion. During a tour of Britain, the band were booked to play a special show at Swansea's Top Rank bingo hall for local medical staff. As the band took to the stage, they noticed that something was wrong with the PA system. Les explained to the audience that they were going to fix the problem before starting. He then took a microphone in his hand to test it. Somehow, the power supply had become misdirected and the mic was live. Les was immediately killed by a massive electric shock.

Alex was devastated by his brother's death. Instead of turning him away from music, however, the loss led him to tap into the driven, manic side of his character. For the rest of his career, he would drive himself harder than ever before, putting everything into his performances. This grief-driven energy would in the end prove self-destructive, but in 1972 it was the source of the greatest period of Alex's career.

17.
GLASGOW VOICES:
AMANDA MACKINNON

Sprite-like and hairclipped, Amanda Mackinnon was the distinctive vocalist of Bis. I say 'was', because the 'sprite' image of the first Bis album, *The New Transistor Heroes*, has long been replaced by a more mature, graceful and somewhat battle-hardened persona (although the hairclip has recently been reinstated). The past tense also sadly applies to Bis, which is now no more (although the same personnel ride again under the banner Data Panik). Amanda's career so far is described in her own words on the Bis website as 'a rollercoaster of stardom and obscurity'. In under a decade, she has gone from Glasgow schoolgirl to pop wonder kid to call-centre worker to radio DJ to pop survivor. She is a fine example of what Glasgow has a lot of, someone who's in it for the love of it, even when much of 'it' is pretty tough.

Why did Bis have to come to an end?
Me, John and Steven decided to end the Bis thing because we'd got to the third album and ever since the first one everything's gone slightly downhill, success-wise anyway – the quality was going up, but the success was going down. Record labels were funnier towards us, weren't picking up on the options, publishing didn't pick up on the option either, so we were sort of stranded by a lot of people. The third album [*Return to Central*] was really hard to get a label for actually. Eventually we got a label whose attitude I don't care for. It went in the shops at a really expensive price, they didn't give us any money to properly tour it or anything. It was a bit of a disaster so we thought 'Right, that's it.'

It's a great album.
Well that's the thing, a lot of people say so. I still listen to it to this day. It sort of saddens me, but it's a nice ending to the whole ten years of Bis. So we thought, the original Bis fans don't really get that we've moved on, we're not this wee cheesy little punky band that we started out as. Ten

years is a long time in music and you want to change, so we just thought right, we'll do a last tour. We did it, kind of not really thinking what we were doing – it's like maybe if you've just split up with a partner or something, you're not really thinking what you're doing at the time. Then there was maybe a lot of regret afterwards and we were getting frustrated not being in music anymore, because we had been from our teenage years into our twenties. We'd always said that we would start a new band, but over a year had passed and we still hadn't done it and we started to get very nervous. I got a job doing a radio show to pay my bills. John and Steven own a recording studio, so whenever they don't have client in, I'm in. I finish work at 1 pm and go there for the rest for the rest of the day. We did a lot of the Data Panik songs a while ago, but now we're just properly, properly getting into it. It's really exciting and we really want to go for it. We now have eighteen songs, with about four that are completely finished and that we won't touch again.

How's the radio show going?
I'd always rather be on the other side – being the person in the band, but I've had to do call-centre rubbish before to pay bills, so to be involved in music is fantastic. I'm in there from nine till one, Monday to Friday, so I've worked out that, if I finish at one, I can still make a sound check in London. It could be a lot worse, the station used to be pretty much a dance station and a lot of R&B stuff, which I really don't like at all, but now we get the Kaiser Chiefs and the Futureheads in the show and I'm pretty happy. It's not a bad job.

What should we expect from Data Panik?
I cannot wait to hear what people say. People ask me what does it sound like, and I don't really know until people start telling me what they think. One of the songs on the double A-side was one that we wrote towards the end of Bis, it's been around that long, so it's changed a lot. I suppose it's just, I don't know, a harder Bis. Better written, better sung, better production, more care into the sounds. Real drums, which makes a difference.

What do you think about the Glasgow scene at the moment?
Glasgow's been strong for a long time, so it's about time it got a bit of

attention. We're used to seeing people around us going out and doing well, Travis or whoever. Alex actually put on the first ever Bis gig in the old 13TH Note. So I've known Alex for a long, long time. He's someone who's been doing music longer than me, so he deserves to have something good happen. And it couldn't happen to anyone nicer than those guys, he's just a genuinely lovely, lovely guy. I hated it when Bis got successful and we got a lot of bitchiness going on in our hometown, because people had been doing it a lot longer than we had, we were seventeen and eighteen and going on *Top of the Pops* and people didn't really like that. So you kind of really get to know who you're real friends are, who's really supportive. The people who are working in Monorail just now have been ultra-supportive since the beginning and will always treat us well, but there are some places you walk into in Glasgow and you get whispering and people being weird.

Can the Glasgow scene be bitchy?
I just think everybody's different, I suppose. I think probably Franz Ferdinand are probably getting it as well. You start getting some success and people are just 'Huh, what's going on there' and making bitchy comments. I mean it was only a month or two ago I was sitting in here [Mono], Alex came in after being on a big tour and came right over and started speaking to me, asking me what I'd been up to. That is just lovely, for someone to not change. He'd maybe deserve the criticism if he'd gone on to be successful and changed as a person and started being a bit arsy and not so nice to people who'd been supportive of him, but he's not. He's a completely genuine guy. I think the three of us were kind of the same, where we didn't change – even when we were on *Top of the Pops*, we were still living with our parents. So, I don't think we changed, anyway. And people turned around and said we were an embarrassment to Scotland and stuff, it wasn't very nice.

Was that in the press?
Yeah. You're going to get it with everything, that good and bad press. That's why this time, once again we're really proud of the music, I'm really enjoying it, if nothing happens with it, OK, fair enough, but I'm loving making it, I love being in the studio with them in the afternoon, it just feels like the most natural thing to be doing, and I think no matter

what age I am I'm still going to be working with them. We did 13 songs for a BBC cartoon that's just started to be shown called BB3B, it's on BBC One on Saturday mornings and Tuesdays. We did 13 songs, one for each episode and then the theme tune, and we're characters in the cartoon. It took ages to do. They took photos of us and just made wee drawings up, and it's got the stripes in my hair and everything and little long, thin legs – I don't where they came from! It says Bis on the drum kit – they've given us a drummer just so it makes sense to the kids. Seeing as Bis is over, I don't really care, they can do what they want. It was a good job, trusted with being songwriters, so I was quite honoured to be asked to do stuff like that.

Have you had any other projects on the go?
Yeah, I had The Kitchen and Steven and John had Dirty Hospital. While we're making either Bis songs or Data Panik songs we always have our own influences, and you always have this wee bit of frustration inside you saying 'need to make guitar music'. I think that was what I was like towards the end of Bis, *Return to Central* was a very nice album, very emotional and deep, but I just wanted some punky guitar music. I did an album and a few brilliant gigs with Hot Hot Heat and Franz Ferdinand and put the album out on Damaged Goods, which I'd always wanted to do, and then it's over, so I feel quite satisfied. OK, so it didn't sell brilliantly, but I don't care, it was a nice thing to do. John and Steven's thing was their techno project, because that's their underlying little frustration, so they did that and played some really trendy, scary clubs and put songs out on trendy labels, and yeah they're done with that as well now – well, I think they've got into something big in the summer, Pressure at The Arches. But these are just things to be doing on the side, it will never be the same as when we're working together, though, there's just something when we all come together which just seems right. I think that's what makes a band. The thing that everyone always said about Bis, which was really nice, was it wouldn't be Bis if any member left. I think that's just such a compliment, because you think of bands like Snow Patrol, Coldplay or Oasis, if their drummer left and they got someone new it's not going to make a difference to the band; whereas if something happened to one of three of us it's not going to be the same. That's a nice thing.

Do you think that's true of Franz Ferdinand?
Yes. It's funny you say that. You know, most of the four-piece male bands at the moment, say the Killers or someone, you only know the singer or maybe the guitarist or someone. There's very rarely a band like Franz Ferdinand where you know every member. OK, maybe I'm a bit biased because I actually know them, but I think even someone like my sister, who wouldn't know them, would be able to name more than one person in the band. In fact, even my mum knows Alex's name from seeing him on TV, although she thought his name was Franz to begin with. I was watching them on the repeat of them on *Frank Skinner* the other night, and I was looking at them thinking that they're one of these four-piece male bands in which you do recognise each member.

Did you follow any of their early bands?
Yeah, I have loads of Yummy Fur records and stuff with Paul, and Pro Forma stuff – Bis played with Pro Forma. And then for Alex's early bands, oh god, what's that one I've got at home, it was an album they put out that the venue put out, it was called the Kazoo Club, the club night they used to put on. What was that band called... the Blisters! You can tell it's him. I suppose the Amphetameanies stuff as well. You can tell that it's still the same guy writing the songs. It's nice though, you can kind of hear where it's coming from.

You're also managing a band at the moment, the Multiplies.
No 'The', just 'Multiplies.

Sorry.
That's OK. It's a mistake a lot of people make and they joke about it now.

How did that come about?
They recorded in John and Steven's studio. They were talking about looking for a manager and were asking about who managed Bis towards the end. So John and Steven said it was me, and they were like 'Ooh'. They asked me if I wanted to do it. I didn't really know at first because I was really, really busy with all the other stuff and also quite nervous because I didn't know them, I didn't know their music – I'd only ever do something like if it's something I'm completely into. So I met with

them and listened to the music – and was completely blown away. When you get asked in interview after interview what other Glasgow bands are you listening to I would draw a blank a lot of the time, in recent years anyway, so to hear them and be stunned by the sound, I just thought: 'OK, I'm going to give this a go.' I don't expect to be ultra-amazing at it because I've not done it for anyone except my own band before, but I've been now doing it for over a year and they've been doing amazingly well. They've just done their second gig headlining at King Tut's, so I'm now pushing for a wee T In The Park bill for them, which hopefully they'll get. They've played with Scissor Sisters and some pretty good bands, so they're doing really well and I'm really enjoying it. It's a nice wee challenge for me.

They've got an interesting mix of electronic and guitar.
Yeah, I suppose the roughest way of describing them, which everyone keeps calling them, is 'synth-rock', which sounds all right to me. In the same way as saying with Bis you can't replace any member, they're like that: each member is so talented. Their drummer is amazing, he looks so tiny and so wee and he's just a thunder drummer, he's fantastic. And the guitarist, bassist and keyboard player are just stunning, absolutely stunning.

Have they been around in other bands before?
Yeah, two of them were in a band called Texlahoma, and David was in Sputniks Down. They seem so naive, but they're only a few years younger than me, what they've done is so little compared to what I had at that age. I feel like I'm sorting of teaching them, so when they get offered gigs, I have to say 'Well, do you think this is good for the band? I know it's an offer, but is it right?' So it's trying to educate them in a way that I wasn't when I started out, because I was very naive, at least I think I was. But you realise that when it comes to record labels getting in touch, offers for 7-inches, gig after gig and how to afford it when you don't have money as a band, it's a good experience, I think they need it, I think they need a hand. I hope I help them, I hope it works out.

Have you seen any changes in the music scene here?
As a scene, Glasgow is probably still quite similar to the way it was when

we started. The thing that's changed is the whole record industry in general. They don't have as much money, whether it's with the downloading or people just not buying as much any more. They don't give out million-pound advances like we used to hear about. You need to be a giant band – people don't want to take risks on you any more. It's like me trying to explain to Multiplies how it is different, you know, you read about a band like Franz Ferdinand doing well, taking this amount of money, and it's not the way it is. You don't earn a lot from being in a band. The music industry is just a weird, weird thing. And there's not as much press anymore – when I was in the band there was the *Melody Maker*, there was *Select*, there was so much more, and the *NME* wasn't the horrible thing it is now, you could get into it and they would do a nice little feature on small bands, up-and-coming ones. You don't really hear about new music anymore, you have to find that usually on the Internet. The Internet wasn't anything when I was doing the band, there were no MP3s to buy, it's so different as an industry, so I'm just trying to get used to it as well. It's amazing, I was thinking about this the other day, when someone calls up or e-mails, asking for a Multiplies song, a biography or press clippings, you e-mail it – you e-mail the whole lot over. I remember when it was Bis and you had to send something to America or Japan, they got it in a week, now it's just instant. It's fantastic, they don't realise how lucky they are. It was so much harder when I was doing it, I didn't even have a computer when I was doing Bis in the beginning! No e-mail!

Do you get frustrated at the lack of a major record company in Scotland?
It's really, really hard. We really would love a record deal, we'd love an album, we'd like someone else to do the work that they're better at than us – I can only hand stamp so many so many sleeves, that's what I'm good at, but when it comes to getting it into the shops I'm not so great, so I'd love a deal. But the number of people I'd actually send it to in the UK... there's not that many labels. There's places like Domino and Rough Trade and Mute, but apart from that you've got to be a massive, massive band. There are cool labels in Europe and America.

What about using the Internet to release stuff?
This is the first time – I mean for this 7-inch, I'm working out how to

get the songs on the Internet to download for a small fee, which is great when you're doing a limited-edition thing and people from America might not want to pay the postage, so it's making things more available. I'm hoping off the back of this labels will get in touch, just from word of mouth. We're under no pressure, it's not like a band that doesn't have the sort of background we do, where they're really trying for it.

Do you still have a big following in Glasgow? Is this where your core fan base is?
Yeah, I'm amazed, like, when Bis split up, it was nearly two years ago now, I just thought that's it, people will forget and times will move on and all the kind of wee Goths you see hanging about will never have heard of us, because we were before them getting into music, so I just thought, 'Och, that's it, we'll start the new band, people will just think it's a new name, cool.' But as soon as I announced it on the website there was e-mail after e-mail saying 'Oh my god, this has made my year, this is so exciting, I can't believe it.' And it was just like 'Oh my god, do we still mean that much to people' and it sent shivers through me. It made me so excited again to think wow, the three of us being together making music has made someone happy. And I hope we live up to that with the music that they get.

And what about Japan? That was your big market.
I don't think it's anywhere near as crazy, because they move very fast there and so it's just in and out and that's it. I just got an e-mail from a record shop there wanting to order 30 copies of the new 7-inch – I didn't advertise any record shops to get in touch. I'm going there on holiday so I'll soon see what they think.

See if you get mobbed.
I did get recognised last time I was out there – not mobbed, but recognised. They're just like 'Are you playing?'

You've kept your trademark hairclip.
I know, I don't know why I did that. You see, I went for ages without it and then just suddenly went back to it, and I was like 'I think I'm going to get so much shit for this, but ach, sod it, it stops it falling in my face.

So what's next for Data Panik?

What we need to do is finish recording an album's worth. As I said, only four are completely finished and they're very fussy, John and Steven, they like everything to be absolutely perfect. So I think we'll get about 12 recorded, so it's ready if anyone wants to do anything. In the meantime, we start rehearsing them and get them ready to play live, because as soon as I announced the new band we got offers in from London, Bath, Germany to go and play – but we can't yet, we don't know how to do it. So we've got a lot of work on. When we wrote these songs we didn't even think about doing them live. Whereas most bands go to a rehearsal room, jam, write a song and it's recorded as it would be played live, we've always done it differently. That album [a copy of *The New Transistor Heroes* is on the table] was written in the normal, rehearsal room kind of way, but after that it was always written on the computer, so it was written and recorded at the same time. Because they own a studio, there's no time constraint, so we just went in and messed about for day, we don't just say right, we're going in to record this song today. It's very different.

Are there other generations of Scottish musicians that you listen to?

Ones in Glasgow, I'm not so sure about. I mean, I used to like Teenage Fanclub when I was younger, but I was more into American punk bands really. I just liked what I could hear on John Peel or whatever and it was only when we started to get compared to the Rezillos that I listened to them for the first time. I hadn't really heard them. Steven, I think, was into Badgewearer before me, so I heard them through him, but the Rezillos I'd never heard of until someone compared Bis to them.

John Peel played your stuff, didn't he?

Yeah, he was the first person to ever play it. It was so exciting. I remember sitting in Steven's room one night and Yummy Fur came on, and I was like, 'If they can go on the radio, why can't we?' and all of a sudden I just heard 'Der der der da da da' and I was like 'Oh my god!'. I think it was just a cassette I sent him, so it was just unbelievable, the version was probably really bad, it was 'Kill Your Boyfriend', the early version. It was just so exciting. He's made it for so many people. It'll be stuck in their memory forever.

18.
GETTING IT TOGETHER

Some time in the early months of 2002, Mick Cooke, trumpeter with Belle and Sebastian and the Amphetameanies, gave Alex a bass on the condition that he do 'something useful with it'. This incident, along with many other details of events leading to the formation of Franz Ferdinand, has been repeated so many times in interviews with the band and duplicated so many more times on the Internet that it almost seems a piece of myth. Perhaps because the band became so successful so quickly, there were very few titbits available to keep journalists and interviewers interested. The Mick Cooke bass incident does, though, reveal three important things about how and why Franz Ferdinand got together. First, it shows the importance of the surrounding scene as a nurturing environment for the band. Second, it shows that Alex was thinking about starting a band, and that the bass acted as a catalyst for him to set his plans into action. Third, it shows how much luck – or fate – was on their side from the beginning.

Instead of using the bass himself to tag onto an existing band, Alex decided to start a band from scratch. He had not stopped writing songs and he wanted a vehicle through which he could air them to the Glasgow public. He set about persuading his young artist friend Bob Hardy to give music a try. This was a considerable undertaking, and perhaps someone with less self-confidence and even arrogance would not have presumed to turn a friend away from his life's work. Bob was open to persuasion, however, and was eventually convinced enough that he could achieve a legitimate self-expression with a bass as well as with a brush. Alex was already a practised bass player and immediately set about introducing Bob to the world of the bass line. It is testament to Bob's creative flair that he has mastered a solid, dependable approach to an instrument with which he has been completely unfamiliar for most of his life.

Bob and Alex's early joint ventures into music soon revealed that they needed a drummer to add spine to their performances. As with any thriving music scene, good drummers are always in short supply and are usually quickly snapped up. A chance meeting at a party (involving another much mythologized incident, this one involving the theft of a bottle of vodka) brought Nick McCarthy into Alex's sphere of awareness. McCarthy was continuing the development of his flamboyant persona in Glasgow, and was still prone to dressing in outlandish costumes. Reports of a lost circus ringleader wandering the streets of Glasgow turned out to be down to Nick and his latest fashion statement. At the party in question, which he was attending with his girlfriend at the time – a student in the art school in Bob's year – he was wearing a silly enough outfit (full Adam Ant regalia) to draw attention to himself. Although the initial meeting with Alex nearly ended up in a brawl over the vodka bottle, the two eventually turned to talking about their shared love of music. It was a pivotal moment. Nick and Alex are the sort of pair who would either hate each other from the start and forever more, or hate each other and then realise they had a lot in common. As the conversation progressed, they both recognised that each represented what the other needed. To Nick, Alex was someone with the drive, determination and leadership to channel Nick's boundless creative energy into a productive rather chaotic trajectory. To Alex, Nick was a talented and experienced musician who had yet to find his niche. He also claimed to play the drums, which met the embryonic band's most pressing requirement.

With his musical training and background, Nick could have been forgiven for thinking 'drums – how hard can it be?' Unfortunately, it did not take long before it was clear that Nick's 'freestyle' drumming technique would not cut the mustard for the type of band that Alex had in mind. In long and expansive conversations with Bob, Alex had been thrashing out exactly what sort of band he wanted to be in. By the time the band were ready to perform, these ideas had been whittled down into a very clear objective, which was subsequently peddled to curious journalists as the Franz Ferdinand manifesto.

Much of this band identity was informed by Alex's experience in the Glasgow scene, and his knowledge of literally hundreds of bands of differing quality and success. This identity was based as much on what the band didn't like as by what it did like. Any indie-dominated scene can produce a strong whiff of reverse snobbism, in which bands frown on any rival band that is too easy to listen to, too enjoyable and (God forbid!) too successful. Glasgow has its fair share of this sort of point of view, and Alex had grown thoroughly sick of it by the end of his work for the 13TH Note. The bands that shone through were those that simply set out to entertain their audiences. From this came the now famous Franz Ferdinand mission statement: 'Music for girls to dance to.' From the very beginning, even before the beginning, Franz were bent on producing good, homemade pop music, in the tradition of the post-punk bands of the early 1980s.

The band's musical influences were vitally important to the sound that they eventually conspired to create. Although Simon Reynolds might dismiss it as 'record collection rock', [30] Franz Ferdinand were drawing on music that they felt strongly about, and using it to create something wholesome in a music industry that seems increasingly satisfied with gloss without content. Among the key influences on the band were Postcard Records bands and the surrounding Scottish scene of the early 1980s: Orange Juice, Josef K, the Fire Engines and the Associates. With these pioneering bands, Franz Ferdinand shared a dislike of 'rockism': the accepted macho traditions and formulas of live popular music, and a desire to cut a friendlier, less egocentric, more creative, more intelligent path into the future of music. It might, as hostile critics have tirelessly pointed out, have been done before, but that in no way means that it does not need to be done again. Although Franz Ferdinand have shied away from calling their approach to pop music a manifesto, the passion with which they (particularly Alex) talk about their musical goals, and the conviction with which they have reached those goals in their completed songs, points to a clear objective in what they create.

The addition of Nick to the band was an essential step forward, but it did not solve their need for a drummer. However, the songwriting partnership of Kapranos and McCarthy started producing fruit almost immediately. From that day to this, the pair has continued to spend spare time working out tunes and lyrics, producing the core ideas that are then taken to the rest of the band for interpretation. The musical excesses of Alex's Karelia years were now alloyed with Nick's classical and jazz training to produce particularly potent pop tunes and rhythms.

30. Simon Reynolds, *Rip It Up And Start Again*, p. xxviii.

Speaking of rhythms, the final addition to the band was Paul Thompson, who, like Bob, was another happy victim of Alex's powers of persuasion. A sign of that persuasiveness is that Alex managed to lure Paul away from a successful and creative band (Pro Forma), which had just achieved its first record release, and convince him to join a completely unknown venture that hadn't even played a gig yet.

It says something for the tremendous energy with which the band approached their task that, just a couple of months after forming, they had written some of their strongest songs and were ready to test them out on the extremely unforgiving ears of the Glasgow scene. Now thoroughly over-familiar with the Glasgow music circuit, Alex was keen not simply to launch the band onto what very often became a merry-go-round. Instead, the band looked for alternative venues within the city. Looking for alternative spaces is something that might not be common in the music world, but it is a well-established practice in the art world. Glasgow had long developed a strong tradition of artists finding and converting spaces in which to display their work, especially with the focus placed on the unusual and outdoor spaces by the influential Environment Art course of the Fine Art department. In May 2002, six of Bob's fellow students – then in their third year – put on a show of their work in a flat on Sauchiehall Street. The show was called *Girl Art* and lasted only a couple of days, but it demonstrated a determination on the part of the participants to show their work despite their lack of access to the male-dominated established gallery spaces in Glasgow. It also says something for that determination that the six artists involved in the show – Hannah Robinson, Joanne Robertson, Celia Hempton (whose flat was used for the show), Sara Barker, Harriet Tritton and Aleana Egan – are all still practising artists. Hannah Robinson, who now runs the Mary Mary gallery in Glasgow, explained that Franz Ferdinand's involvement in the show came about because Bob was in their year and that 'we wanted a boy band to go with *Girl Art*.' It was just the sort of non-traditional venue that the band had been looking for and, despite jitters about whether they were ready for a live performance after just a few rehearsals, Franz Ferdinand[31] agreed to play. The early songs performed at that show included their first two singles 'Darts Of

31. The band's name had been inspired by a horse called Archduke appearing on a TV racing programme.

Pleasure' and 'Take Me Out'. With the repertoire still on the short side (although miraculously well-advanced considering the time involved) the band ran through it a couple of times. It was another make or break or moment, but all involved seem convinced that they were onto something: girls (and boys) had indeed danced. Another performance followed in June in Nick's abode in the Dumbreck area of the city, to the south of the Clyde, and Franz Ferdinand were on a roll that would take them to global success.

Another landmark performance took place in September, when the band were invited to take part in one of artist Lucy McKenzie's showcases at Flourish Studios on Robertson Street. The Flourish events had been established by Mackenzie in the same grand, red-stone building – which once housed the offices of a well-to-do shipping company – as the renowned Modern Institute. The title of the space refers to the motto of Glasgow City Council: 'Let Glasgow flourish'. Glaswegian Lucy McKenzie had graduated in Fine Art from Dundee's Duncan of Jordanstone College in 1998, her work causing a stir when it was snapped up by art speculator Charles Saatchi. Fame and fortune beckoned in London, but instead McKenzie returned to Glasgow and put her energy into the local – but increasingly internationally renowned – art scene. As well as continuing her art practice, working with the famous Transmission Gallery, she also became involved in various art-music crossover projects. One of these was a collaborative event with artists including Robert Johnston (later of Life Without Buildings) called *Nausea*. Four DJs, McKenzie one of them, worked shifts to create a barrage of noise at painful decibel levels for five hours. The fifty-odd members of the audience endured as much as they could in the interests of exploring the boundaries between enjoyment and endurance. This led to a series of events under the heading *Punish*, some of which were held at McKenzie's Flourish Studios. Her background in music also dated back to before her study in Dundee: she had been one of the founder members of the post-rock group Ganger in 1995. This innovative band, graced with two bassists, a drummer and McKenzie on guitar, looked to the experimental era of Krautrock in the early 1970s, and produced music that proved highly influential in Glasgow (they pre-date Mogwai), but which failed to garner the success it deserved. The band eventually split in 2000, following which bassist Natasha Noramly established Fuck-Off Machete and guitarist Craig B. Aereogramme.

Franz's appearance at the Flourish Studios showcase was their first major booking and their toughest test so far. That the Flourish night was a success is attested to by the fact that the art world invitations kept on coming: Franz's next show took place in Edinburgh in October. Once again, it was through their art world contacts that the invitation came about. In June, a group of Edinburgh artists had put on a group show called *Magnifitat* in a shared flat in the city. As with *Girl Art*, the idea was to make a space for showing work in a city where such spaces were rare and hard for young artists to access. The first *Magnifitat*[32] was a success, and another was arranged for October. It was the opening of this second exhibition, which featured a performance piece by artists Kim Coleman and Susie Green, and work by Annette Knol and Emma Williams, Christo Wallers, Lisa Castagner, Mary Ann Tuckermann and Ilana Mitchell, for which Franz Ferdinand were invited to play.

Following this friendly introduction to live performance – their audiences up to this point were largely made up of friends and were people on the same wavelength as the band – the band braved their first performance in a bona fide music venue. Of course, with Franz Ferdinand's combined Glasgow music scene contacts, they could have arranged to play at almost any of the city's best venues. In the end, it was the newly opened West 13TH on Kelvinhaugh Street in Glasgow's West End that saw the band's first 'real' gig. The new venue was another venture by one of the pillars of the Glasgow music scene, Craig Tannock, the entrepreneur and music missionary behind the 13TH Note venues. West 13TH would subsequently be renamed Stereo to partner another of Tannock's ventures, Mono, a bar, café and music venue in the tradition of the 13TH Note but with its own microbrewery and record shop, Monorail.[33] It seemed fitting that Alex's return to the Glasgow music scene was carried out under the auspices of his former boss.

The next venue the band would appear in, in November, was another milestone. The Vic Bar in the Glasgow School of Art student union had had legendary status for launching the careers of Scottish bands since

32. Magnifitat is still running, as is the Embassy Gallery established in Edinburgh by some of the same collective of artists.

33. Probably the best record shop in the world, seeing as you stand the chance of being served and advised by The Pastels' Stephen Pastel.

time immemorial. It was here that two of Franz Ferdinand's key influences, Orange Juice and Josef K, had played a shared bill in 1979, just before the launch of Postcard Records. Once again, it was friendly territory for the band, and they had been in the audience of the venue many times in the past. Franz's early shows in Glasgow and Edinburgh demonstrate how important their previous experience and wealth of contacts were to their growing success. Rather than plunge straight into the unfriendly ocean of the wider music circuit, they were gently nurtured by a close-knit community within a close-knit scene. This is not to say that they did not come up against their fair share of criticism (much more of which was to come when they started to become successful), but they were more or less surrounded by friends and likeminded audiences who liked what they heard and wanted them to do well. If the band's initial entry into the trials and tribulations of live performance had been unorthodox as far as the music world was concerned, then their next step was positively radical. The Château era was dawning.

19.
RETURN OF THE SAINT

Just over a month after the death of his brother, Alex Harvey took steps to move his career into a higher gear. Since coming under the aegis of Bill Fehilly's Mountain Managements, he had started to build a loyal following in London, but was aware that he was still not where he wanted to be. For the moment, Fehilly was paying more money and attention to his other big act, Nazareth. This band had been regulars at the Burns Howff, but had leapt at the chance to move to London and become professionals. With their fame growing towards the worldwide phenomenon they remain to this day, it was understandable that Fehilly would focus his efforts on them rather than Alex.

Although a popular attraction in the London venues, Alex was now well into his thirties and those analysing his career at the time could have been forgiven for thinking that his best was in the past. Another problem was his band, which was generally viewed as not suitable for the intense, powerful singer. It was with these issues in mind that Fehilly asked one his managers, Eddie Tobin, to find a new band for Alex. At the time, Tobin was managing a Glasgow rock band called Tear Gas, which had risen to considerable fame in Scotland but was now plateauing. The band had even shared the bill with Alex at a Marquee show in early 1972. The idea was put forward of turning Tear Gas into Alex's band. Alex had been impressed enough by what he'd heard at the Marquee to go with the idea, and Tear Gas realised that with their career in decline they had nothing to lose by the union. In June 1972, the two parties met at the Burns Howff for a day-long rehearsal. Energised by finally having a reliable band behind him, Alex launched into the rehearsal with his old fervour. The whole thing clicked, and the Sensational Alex Harvey Band was born.

The first two SAHB albums, recorded in 1972 and 1973, seem to capture everything that Glasgow had been musically and much of what was to come. The raw ingredients of R&B, soul and rock 'n' roll are all there, together with hints of the punk explosion to come in a few years time. The live presence of the SAHB was something new, thrilling and sometimes even terrifying. With a sense of the theatre of music garnered from his years in *Hair*, Alex put together shows that were choreographed to deliver the maximum impact on the audience. The band frequently wore costumes, guitarist Zal Cleminson even adopting a look inspired by the Joker from the Batman comics. Alex developed a number of on-stage personas, from Jesus Christ complete with styro-foam crucifix to Adolf Hitler. This bizarre but entertaining approach to performance demonstrated Alex's continuing refusal to deal in mere 'rockism', as the post-punk generation would come to label the bundle of preconceived ideas about rock music. The SAHB never just went through the motions, hiding behind the cardboard mystique that 'rock gods' place between themselves and their audience. Alex craved reaction, whether positive or negative, from his audience, and his performances led some critics to be impressed but somewhat scared by him: an early review in the *NME* described Alex's impact: 'Evil is the best word to describe the demonic presence of Harvey himself.' And it wasn't just the audience and music press who were scared; other members of the band had to get used to Alex's pre-performance workout, which involved standing on his head and then repeatedly screaming 'Cunts!' at a mirror.

This last and greatest period of Alex Harvey's fame lasted from 1972 until 1977, when the SAHB split up. Incapable of not performing, Alex got another band together, this time called simply the Alex Harvey Band. He continued to perform with them and subsequent recruits, despite deteriorating health caused by his alcohol intake and relentless schedule, right up until his death on tour in 1982. In a fitting piece of synchronicity, Alex's late heyday coincided with another resurgence of interest in R&B and soul in Glasgow. The Detroit sound of Motown was all the rage once again, although this time it was DJs armed with sacks of imported records rather than bands as soul juke boxes as it had been in the 1960s. It was to describe this 1970s resurgence of interest in black American music that Falkirk-born journalist Dave Godin coined the phrase 'Northern Soul', although Glasgow had never really ended its love affair with the music since it first landed in the late 1950s.

20.

TO THECHÂTEAU BORN

xhibitions such as *Girl Art* and *Magnifitat* were examples of the well-established art world practice of seeking out alternative spaces in which to work and display art. For Franz Ferdinand, immersed as they were in the crossover scene between the music and art communities, the idea of finding a space for them to practise and 'display' their work must have seemed an obvious idea. One of the reasons for Glasgow's thriving creative scene is the affordability of rent in the city, [34] as well as the many vacant buildings left over from the glory days of Glasgow's industrial and trading peak. The band had previously been using Nick's Hamilton Avenue house as a base of operations, as it had the greatest floor space of their respective homes, but this was not feasible as a regular venue or practise space. Nick had taken to touring Glasgow on his bicycle on the lookout for interesting buildings that could be used as performance and practise spaces.

In the autumn of 2002, he and Alex came across a strong candidate. Just a few minutes' walk from the city centre, across the Glasgow Bridge, lay a mostly empty, six-storey art-deco workshop and warehouse, set a few yards off Bridge Street. Local inquiries soon resulted in an informal agreement with the landlord, and Franz Ferdinand were given keys to the sixth floor. The building was in a serious state of decay, was the home to a large colony of pigeons (and other assorted fauna), had no working heating or lighting system, and most of its windows were broken. Pigeon droppings had in some areas built up over many years to form a layer many inches thick. A lot of work would be needed before it would be fit for use as a long-term place of work. However, excited by their find, the band laid on an initial event using some of the objects they found scattered about their new home. The result was a Sports and Leisure night, featuring airgun marksmanship, rowing-machine racing (with the rowing machines installed on trolleys), and horseback riding

---

34. Although prices are now rising fast in the artist-colonised Saltmarket area.

on an exercise horse (the sort used by gymnasts). The event was fun, but it simply served to raise the band's ambitions even further. The ironically named Château could become an incredible venue. Before this dream could be realised, however, the space would need some serious cleaning and renovation.

It was far too large a task for the band and their friends, so they called in the experts. Nick's flatmate, artist and events organiser Robb Mitchell, agreed to help them out. He in turn managed to interest one of Glasgow's most innovative art collectives in the project. Switchspace had started in 1999 as a series of exhibitions set up by artists Sorcha Dallas and Marianne Greated in Sorcha's Cranworth Street flat. Moving out from the flat in the following years, Switchspace utilised a number of venues around Glasgow. Some of these required considerable renovation work in order to be usable, and so Marianne and Sorcha moved around the city like a pair of art angels transforming mucky interiors into pristine white gallery spaces. This was just the sort of experience Robb Mitchell needed to call upon in order to open the Château. While Franz and friends inhabited the sixth floor, installed equipment, lighting and performance area, on the floor below the Switchspace team, together with the participating artists, moved in to turn the dilapidated rooms into a contemporary art space. By the night of the opening event on 6 December 2002, lighting had been set up, many kilogrammes of pigeon crap had been removed, walls had been painted white, and the artists' work had been installed.

The regular crowd turned out to see Glasgow's latest art space, intrigued by the music-led nature of the project. As the hundreds of guests arrived, they clambered up the crumbling staircase to the now-gleaming exhibition space. The contributing artists included Neil Bickerton and Lorna Macintyre, Karla Black, Kim Coleman and Susea Green (of *Magnifitat*), Paul Embleton, Alex Frost, Lotte Gertz, Emily Richardson and Hayley Tompkins (sister of Life Without Buildings singer and performance artist, Sue Tompkins). Then, as the clock struck nine, the guests made their way to the sixth floor where a curious sight awaited them. Not having access to traditional stage lighting, and not wishing to perform in the cold, sterile atmosphere produced by standard fluorescent tubes, Franz Ferdinand and co had installed a series of sun beds, which they had found in the warehouse, along the walls of the music room. As the performance got under way, these flicked on and off, creating an eerie glow. Along with an informal bar and a makeshift PA system, everything that was needed for a night of music and dance had been assembled.

Along with Franz themselves, Park Attack, Uncle John and Whitelock, and Scatter had been booked. The last in the list was the freestyle jazz ensemble that Nick still occasionally played double bass for. Park Attack[35] remains one of Glasgow's great musical gems, playing music in the same general area as Pro Forma, but heavier, dirtier, grungier. Long-time favourites of the art crowd in Glasgow, Park Attack are a one-band musical movement, a movement they've christened 'What Wave', with its roots in the brief 'No Wave' phenomenon in late-1970s New York. Combining detuned guitars, screaming/whining vocals and rumbling percussion with primitive-sounding electronic beeps, Park Attack perform songs with inspired titles such as 'If Music Be The Food Of Love Then I Think I Just Threw Up', and 'I'm Gonna Storm The Citadel Of Your Womanhood'. Even more than Franz themselves, their sound suited the arty yet gritty ambience of the Château's opening night perfectly. Uncle John and Whitelock have long been at the top of the pile of the Glasgow music scene and, like Park Attack, have invented a musical genre all of their own. Crossing country and western with bluesy punk, the band come across like fatally heroin-addicted 1920s blues musicians who have been raised from the dead, force fed Scottish punk records (orally), pushed onto a stage and told to perform. It's a magnificent sound that has to be heard to be believed, and once again highly apt for an event that was fast developing over-tones of a Chicago speakeasy.

The crowds continued to assemble, but among those wanting in were a group of less than welcome guests. A team from the Strathclyde Police had been despatched to find the source of an outrageous noise emanat-ing from the Bridge Street area. Complaints had been coming from res-idents on and off for weeks (about as long as Franz Ferdinand had been rehearsing in the Château) and police had been driven to distraction try-ing to track down where the noise was coming from. The Château build-ing is set back from the main street and there is no obvious way into the

35. Park Attack are Lorna Gilfedder, Tom Straughan and Rob Churm.

building. Police spent some time milling around outside trying to work out how to get in. Eventually, they located the innocent-looking door between the shop fronts on Bridge Street that allows access to the warehouse. At first, just a small group of police entered the venue, but when they saw the number of people inside they quickly called for back-up. It must have brought back bad memories of illegal gatherings in warehouse spaces during the rave era, but luckily they were dealing with a crowd less interested in trashing buildings than renovating them and turning them into art galleries. Alex presented himself as the organiser of the event and was duly arrested and carted off to the local nick for questioning. Numerous bylaws had been broken, including health and safety, noise, and illegal alcohol sales, but Alex managed to charm his interrogators and he was quickly released.

Although the police had left it late enough for all concerned to have enjoyed the event, it was now clear that the glories of the Château were not a long-term solution to the band's need for a rehearsal and performance space. The search for a new home began. Switchspace also withdrew from the Château: being an officially registered organisation in receipt of Scottish Arts Council funding they could not risk being involved with a building with the continuing health and safety issues of the Château. However, Robb Mitchell has continued to organise the redevelopment of the space together with other artists who use the Château as a studio/exhibition centre. The Château also lives on in the concept of art-flavoured music events organised by Mitchell, two of which have since been held in London, many others in Glasgow.

21.

GLASGOW VOICES: ANDY MILLER

Andy Miller is the producer at the heart of Chem19, the recording studio run by the Delgados-owned label Chemikal Underground. He is held in a great deal of affection and respect by Glasgow's musicians, having earned himself a reputation for capturing a raw, honest, live sound in the studio that gives his recordings a powerful quality of presence. The proof of Miller's gentle genius for getting the best out of his studio clients lies not in his words but in his many records, among which are works by Arab Strap, Magoo, Desert Hearts, Mogwai, the Delgados, Sons And Daughters and Life Without Buildings. I visited the studio in Hamilton just outside Glasgow while Andy was taking a brief break from recording the Mother And The Addicts' debut album, *Take The Lovers Home Tonight*.

Natasha Noramly (Fuck-Off Machete) was saying that you helped her learn how to play bass and sing at the same time. Do you take a hands-on approach with all your clients?
I kind of approach everything the same way; I try to put 100 per cent into getting the best-sounding record that can be made. I like to emphasise performance and really push that as the key to the recording – it's about getting across an enjoyment of playing and capturing that performance, that magic, the thing that you can't actually totally speak about. When it's there you totally hear it and when it's not it's quite obvious that it's missing. I try to gear everything towards that and try whatever I need to do with the band to get that. At the same time, I also think it's good to approach everything individually – the essence of each band is fundamentally different.

How did you get into this?
I kind of stumbled into it. I've been doing it for a long time now. Started off recording a few bands, I've always kind of done this, but it went so

well, people said it was the best recording they'd ever done sort of thing, and things just kind of followed on. It's a fantastic job to have. There's been a lot of different bands through here over the years, so musically it's quite broad. I like honest music and there is a lot of that. I relate with a lot of the bands from around here.

Glasgow is a very self-sufficient place, but do you think it suffers from not having a major label?
I think Chemikal Underground, who I work for, have done a fantastic job and have really inspired me – I've actually started a label [Gargleblast Records], put out a couple of singles last year, we're going to be putting out the albums this years, so I'm actually in the process of mixing one of them today, a band called De Rosa. I think Sam, who I'm rehearsing today from Mother And The Addicts, is a strong return to form for CU.

Who else is on the radar?
My Latest Novel are a band who have really caught my attention. They're coming in to do an album pretty soon, over the next month or so, so I'm really looking forward to that, I worked with the guys on a couple of things quite recently. I think their approach to music, again, it's got that really honest quality to it, which will be how we approach their recording.

I saw them at the Château evening at the ICA.
Did you enjoy it?

Yes, it just hits you because it's got that ...
Yeah, it's got that really nice fragility to it, but at the core totally strong, I kind of like that.

It seems to have the gloss of what's going on in the pop world at the moment taken off.
Yeah, absolutely.

You did the Life Without Buildings album.
Life Without Buildings are one of my favourite bands.

Mine as well.

I was speaking to Sue, who's a great friend of mine, she's an amazing person, it would be great to see Sue doing something else. Robert from Life Without Buildings is going to be in next week playing on the Desert Hearts record, which again is recording on my label. Recording the Life Without Buildings album was a fantastic experience for me. It was really kind of full on, but we had a fantastic time and at the end of the day I think we made an astounding record.

How did the performance happen? Sue's vocal performance sounds free-flowing and improvised.

It does, but a lot of it is fairly structured. The way she writes is the way she speaks, which is fantastic, she can actually put her personality into an e-mail, which is quite a difficult one, but I think that's just how her whole mind works. Sue's one of the best lyricists I ever came across, I find it totally inspirational. I don't think anything like it exists. It's a real shame that she isn't doing something with music just now, but hopefully...

How does a band end up in your studio?

Generally, it's through other records we have done attracting people to come and record here. People like the sound of the records so they want as much as possible their record to sound the same way.

You mentioned Mother And The Addicts, who else has been in recently?

The Delgados just finished their album earlier on in the summer and Arab Strap are actually in the process of finishing off their album just now. It's been a hive of activity late. Actually, it's always, always busy.

22.
POP RESURRECTIONS

Throughout the 1970s, rock music underwent a series of trans-formations. Many progressive musicians were growing increasingly frustrated by the confines imposed by the American rock 'n' roll tradition. What had started as a combination of various, vibrant sub-cultural movements had now been absorbed fully into the mainstream. By the end of the 1960s, many felt that rock was tired, going nowhere and propped up on a series of dubious clichés. Ironically, this was much the same stifling cultural climate that had spawned rock 'n' roll in the first place; as the 1970s dawned, musicians looked for a way forward, a way to rebel and break out of American-style rock music. Like an outbreak of chickenpox, this rebellion appeared concurrently in many different places, including within the USA itself.

A number of means were employed to make a shift forward; one of them was to look back. In an early form of what Simon Reynolds describes in his history of post-punk as present-day 'record collection rock',[36] bands looked to the music they had admired themselves to try to find the point where it all went wrong and then start again from that moment. In a sense, this describes Glasgow's constant returning to the original black American music from which rock 'n' roll had been forged. They were constantly ripping it up and starting again. However, it would be in Edinburgh, rather than Glasgow, that the first successful attempt was made to edit out the unwanted bits of musical history in this way. Before we get to the Rezillos, though, we'll deal with the other way of moving forward: not travelling in time, but in space.

In 1976, after completing his *Station To Station* album, David Bowie left his home in Los Angeles and moved to Berlin. This wasn't just an attempt to get away from the drug-heavy lifestyle he had fallen into in the States, he was also setting out on a quest to find a new sort of music. It had been the new electronic sounds being created by the crassly

---

36. Simon Reynolds, *Rip It Up And Start Again*, p. xxviii.

named 'Krautrock' movement in Germany that had caught his ear, particularly the 1974 Kraftwerk album *Autobahn*, the title track of which had been a hit in the UK and USA. The impact of the German sound clicked with Bowie's sense of having come to the end of the road with American-based music.

The year before *Station To Station* had seen Bowie flirting with the end of his own music and that of American rock as a whole with *Young Americans*. With it, Bowie deliberately crafted what he described as 'plastic soul', a derogatory term used in the 1960s by black American musicians of what were seen as copycat bands such as the Rolling Stones. Recording the album in Philadelphia with black backing vocalists including Luther Vandross, Bowie produced a strangely sterile, plastic sound. The album, though commerically successful, marked a low ebb in Bowie's personal life.

In the title of *Station To Station*, Bowie refers to the Stations of the Cross that are used by Christians as waypoints of remembrance of Christ's crucifixion. The reference reflects the suffering that Bowie was enduring at the time, but by using it he also paints himself as a messianic figure whose suffering is not in vain. *Station To Station* shows the considerable influence of electronic music, while retaining the superficial structures of American-style rock. It contains within it both the end of one phase and the beginning of another, not just for Bowie, but for the avant-garde of popular music.

In a sense, Bowie achieved his messianic mission: by travelling to Germany and immersing himself in the techniques being used there; by not abandoning his R&B foundations but combining them with new musical forms; by passing this still relatively obscure music up into a wider circle of influence. Through the connector of Bowie, Western pop music fed into the sounds that would show it the way forward.

The German music that Bowie was drawn to was made by a relatively small yet diverse group of bands who were moving into exciting new territory from the late 1960s and through the 1970s. Most famous among these is Kraftwerk, whose work had turned Bowie's head in the first place, but they were one of a number of equally innovative bands whose music still sounds contemporary today. Where the prog rock trend of the late 1960s had moved into the territory of classical music and floundered, the new German sound came at the problem (of where to go next with music) from a different angle. Instead of churning out cod-classical without any real knowledge of classical music, German bands looked to living avant-garde composers for inspiration.

In fact, classical composers had faced a similar crisis (the end of music) earlier in the twentieth century, in answer to which composers entered the chaos of atonality and new musical scales such as Arnold Schönberg's 12-note serial method. In the wake of this 'end of music', composers were liberated from centuries of convention to explore new avenues. One of these was the use of newly invented electronic instruments and recording techniques. In the 1950s, the Paris-based Musique Concrete group, which included pioneering technician and composer Pierre Schaeffer, and composers Oliver Messiaen, Pierre Boulez and Karlheinz Stockhausen, invented instruments with which to place real ('concrete') sounds in musical contexts, in the process transforming both the sound and the music. They also invented techniques such as looping, which would go on to be hugely influential in themselves. By the end of the 1960s, the influence of this electronic avant-garde had soaked in, and began to cross over into rock music. It surfaced not just in Europe, but also in America where composers such as John Cage, Steve Reich and Morton Subotnick used electronic techniques, as did experimental jazz composer Milton Babbitt (in his 1964 *Ensembles for Synthesizer*) and pop musician Jean Jacques Perrey (1968's *The Amazing New Electronic Pop Sound*).

It was in Germany during the 1970s, however, where the most convincing and influential merging of traditional R&B rhythms with electronic sound modes was achieved. The bands – Kraftwerk, Neu!, Can, Tangerine Dream, Faust, Cluster, to name the most influential – produced sounds and vocal techniques that were utterly new and in many ways shocking to the comfortable established order of rock. Rock had been audibly torn to pieces and reconstructed in a new, gleaming form. It was this electronic revolution that Bowie, especially in his two 1977 albums *Low* and *"Heroes"*, brought to the attention of the generation of musicians that would go on to create post-punk. Brian Eno, with his 1973 collaboration with King Crimson guitarist Robert Fripp *No Pussyfooting*, and his 1975 solo work *Discreet Music*, as well as his work on the two Bowie albums, was another electronic prophet to post-punk and subsequent New Pop.

Before this graceful, constructive shift to the future could sink into the wider US and UK consciousness, however, a more brutal and destructive one erupted. Punk sprang from the same feelings of dissatisfaction with rock 'n' roll that had brought Bowie and Eno to Berlin, but if the latter's answer was carefully to graft what was salvageable and worthwhile onto a new trunk, punk's was to cut the whole tree down, have a bonfire and stomp on the ashes. Punk was not a just a musical movement, but also an expression of the tedium and powerlessness felt by a whole generation. While punk flared briefly and died, the impact of the new electronic music was far more lasting; it continues to provide a crucial impetus to pop music today, which is perhaps why it still sounds so utterly new. Anyone listening to Neu!'s eponymous first album for the first time could be forgiven for thinking that it was created last week, rather than in 1972.

The Edinburgh-based Rezillos' chosen method for breathing new life into pop music in the mid-1970s was to resuscitate music from the previous decade. Looking to the Velvet Underground and the Stooges as their source of power, the Rezillos combined the trashy sound of those bands with a 1960s sci-fi image to create a colourful, vibrant band that prefigured post-punk rather than reflected the punk movement itself. Forming from the ashes of a band called the Knutsford Dominators in 1976, the Rezillos consisted of recent students of the Edinburgh College of Art. Krautrock had fed on the legacy of avant-garde composers, and the Rezillos took the aesthetic sensibilities they had honed at art school to create a strikingly different image and sound that nevertheless was right for the moment. What had been termed 'art' or 'prog rock' aspired to the nature of art, but without enough conceptual substance – it simply tried to sound 'arty'. The German innovators, together with their evangelists such as Eno and Bowie, were expressing in a popular form ideas that had been around in avant-garde circles for decades.

The Rezillos were not operating in a vacuum as pioneers of sub-culture in Edinburgh. As well as the College of Art where they had studied, by 1976 the city had developed a small but potent contemporary art scene that stood in stark contrast to the traditional, fusty atmosphere of the Scottish capital. Early northern evangelists for ideas-based art, such as Alexander Moffat and Richard Demarco, set up galleries at which local and international artists could display the type of work that publicly funded galleries would simply not consider. Demarco opened his first gallery in 1966, while still serving as Vice-Chairman of the experimental Traverse Theatre, the same year that the New 57 Gallery – in which Moffat was involved – opened. The latter instigated a rotating committee system of artists to run it, a model that was later adopted by the Transmission Gallery in Glasgow.

The idea of both galleries was to maintain the international attention afforded Edinburgh during the Festival all year round, to bring Scottish artists to a wider audience but also to bring internationally renowned artists to Scotland. The most significant international artist to come to Glasgow as the result of these efforts was Joseph Beuys. On the invitation of Richard Demarco, Beuys made his first visit to Scotland in the summer of 1970. This visit strengthened the existing links between the Edinburgh College of Art and the Düsseldorf Kunsthalle and Akademie where Beuys taught and resulted in an exhibition of contemporary German art at the College. Later the same summer, Beuys returned to Edinburgh during the Festival and installed *The Pack*[37] at the College and performed an Action[38] *called Celtic (Kinloch Rannoch) – The Scottish Symphony* (this was four hours long and was performed twice a day for four days). Beuys developed a close affinity with Scotland and returned six more times over the coming decade. The presence of such a superstar of the contemporary art world could not but raise the profile of Scottish art, in the eyes of the world as much as in the local artists' own estimation.

It was inevitable that some of this growing confidence in the art scene would rub off onto music in the city. The Rezillos were the first expression of this crossover of energy and ideas. Their first single, 'Can't Stand My Baby' was released in 1977 on the Edinburgh-based Sensible label owned by their manager Lenny Love. It was enough to reach the ears of Sire Records boss Seymour Stein, who was on a talent-spotting trip to the UK at the time (he also snapped up the Undertones while he was at it) and the successful album *Can't Stand the Rezillos* was released on Sire in 1978. They split up before the year was out.

Meanwhile, while punk was already sputtering out in the rest of the country, it was still struggling to gain a foothold in Glasgow.

37. Created in 1969, The Pack consists of a pack of sleds carrying roll-up blankets, electric torches and pieces of fat apparently caught in the act of rushing out of the back of a Volkswagen van.

38. Actions or Happenings are a type of performance artwork.

23.
GO STRAIGHT TO JAIL

Despite their eviction from the Château at the beginning of the month, December 2002 proved to be Franz Ferdinand's busiest gigging month to date. By this time, under six months since their debut in Celia Hempton's flat, the buzz that would carry the band to a worldwide audience had started to take effect. They were the hot ticket within Glasgow, and news was spreading further afield about the brilliant band who were putting the guitar back into pop. Music fans from the south started appearing at Franz shows, among them A&R men coming to check out the band that was already making big waves. Another show at West 13TH – now rechristened Stereo – was shared with Uncle John and Whitelock, with further performances at the Transmission Gallery party held at Nice 'n' Sleazy, and another invitation to one of Lucy McKenzie's Flourish Studios events. As Christmas approached, Franz Ferdinand were beginning to realise that they were onto something big. There was a chance that they might not be destined to be just another Glasgow band. With this possibility in mind, a visit to London was arranged for the following February. In the meantime, it was time to visit friends and family for Christmas.

Nick's search for a new home for the band continued unabated. Eagerly pedalling through the Glasgow winter gloom, he started to explore the east end of the central city area. He had come to know this area well in the last year, as Alex's flat, where Nick frequently went to work on songs, was in the eastern district of Dennistoun. Just south of Dennistoun lies a district called Bridgeton, near the Barras area and the Barrowland Ballroom. Cycling up a fairly rundown street one day, Nick came across a magnificent red brick Victorian building at 100 Tobago Street. After enquiring with the garage owner and scrap dealer who worked next to the building, Nick learned that the building was unoccupied and a simple agreement gained him access. It turned out to be a complex of buildings covering almost an acre that had been the offices of Bridgeton CID (Criminal Investigation Department). When it was first built, the complex had been a sort of one-stop criminal centre: you could be arrested, tried, jailed, and executed (by hanging) without getting wet.

As far as Franz Ferdinand's needs were concerned, the space was perfect. It was self-enclosed enough for their rehearsals not to disturb neighbours too much, and also contained a courtroom space that was perfect for putting on shows. What was more, many of the cells still had barred gates so that the band could store and lock up their equipment. In addition to the bass guitar donated by Mick Cooke in the very beginning, the band had gradually assembled the equipment they needed to out on live shows. One of the most exciting finds had been a classic Hagström P46 guitar, [39] which Alex had spotted in a Glasgow charity shop. The guitar was immediately recognisable to Alex as Brian Ferry sports one on the cover of Roxy Music's second album, *For Your Pleasure*. It was the perfect symbol of what Franz Ferdinand were about and Alex had to have it. Luckily, the shop manager was unaware of the cultural importance of the instrument and handed it over for a small price. Subsequently, Nick has also tracked down a Hagström and the band have now become the (now defunct) company's best advertisers since Aerosmith waved their Hagström axes around.

Once again, Nick's flatmate Robb Mitchell was called in to help turn the Tobago Street space into an art and music venue. Following the Christmas break, work started in earnest. Artists were allocated individual cells

39. Hagström was once Sweden's most important music company but it wasn't originally known for its guitars. When Albin Hagström set up in business in 1921, he started by importing accordions, and within a few years he was making his own. In 1958, the company decided to get into the increasingly popular market for electric guitars and amps. Coming from their unconventional background, Hagström's first guitars looked like nothing that had been seen before. The body was hollow, so the guitar could be played as an acoustic, and the whole body and even the fingerboard were covered in a thick layer of sparkle plastic. Colours were bright blues, reds, golds... usually with contrasting mother-of-pearl on the top, neck and back of the guitar. More accordion than electric guitar. The other striking feature of the Hagström electrics was their replaceable pickup assemblies, which fitted onto a chrome panel complete with all the controls. The whole thing looked like a perfect classic 1950s design, and Hagströms were soon being exported to other countries, including the USA, where they were sold under the Goya brand. The guitar was called a 'Sweetone' and came in Standard and Deluxe versions. The interchangeable pickup panels meant that the dealers could offer lots of different options. The guitars could be played as acoustics with a simple soundhole surround or with different pickup combinations: a P24 had two pickups and a P46 had four pickups with six buttons, giving lots of switching options. The Hagström business closed its doors in 1981, but once estimated that some 800,000 musicians had played their guitars, including Elvis Presley, David Bowie, The Beatles, ABBA, Frank Zappa, ZZ Top, Genesis and Jimi Hendrix.

around the central court area and installed their work ready for opening night on the 15 February of a show called *Cells Out*. This time, artists included Sara Barker, Joanne Robertson and Celia Hempton of *Girl Art* fame, Kim Coleman (*Magnifitat*), and Rob Churm of Park Attack, among others. Meanwhile, Franz Ferdinand prepared the courtroom as a performance space. They then invited Scatter and Country Teasers to share the 'stage'. Country Teasers originated in Edinburgh, but had found their spiritual home in Glasgow. Bandleader Ben Wallers had created a totally deranged style of music and lyrics that was sharply and blackly ironic, somewhat in the tradition of Mark E Smith and without much of a trace of country (thus, perhaps, the tease). Franz were and continue to be admirers of Wallers' *oeuvre*. Hordes of art and music aficionados braved the wilds of the East End to explore the intriguing space and watch the bands on offer. Although the police did eventually turn up, they were not as alarmed as they had been at the Château opening (perhaps they felt more at home), eventually simply turning the power off instead of hauling Alex off for questioning.

Unlike the break-up of the Château, which was effectively an eviction notice as far as Franz Ferdinand were concerned, this time the band stayed put. The Bridgeton jail continued to be their base of operations and official home until the end of 2004. The space – and their equipment – was kept safe by the artists who had also permanently moved into the complex, using the cells as studios.

The move to the jail marks the start of a distinct new phase in Franz Ferdinand's rise. Music industry interest had been piqued, and Franz Ferdinand were just beginning to appear on the radar of London-based record companies. In order to give them a better view of what was on offer, Franz headed south for the first time at the end of February. They took with them Ben Wallers under his solo guise of the Rebel. Two shows followed, at Cherry Jam (Porchester Road) and the Arts Café (Commercial Street), with DJs Mairead and Tabitha – also known as the Queens of Noize – joining them in the Arts Café. Although not major venues, they were just the right size to showcase Franz to the record company reps in the audience. These two London performances set the music industry alight. Franz Ferdinand were indie and guitar-based but poppy enough that you could dance to their songs. Any A&R man hearing 'Take Me Out' for the first time can't have helped being sent into a frenzy of excitement, with the sound of cash tills ringing in his ears. Franz Ferdinand had gone to London to let the music industry hear what they were made of; from now on, it was the music industry that would do the travelling.

Returning victorious to Glasgow, Franz left the London-centric record industry in a fervour. Back at home, they carried on with business as usual, playing at the Barfly on the River Clyde on 12 March and preparing for a gig under the auspices of the Glasgow School of Art on 26 March. It was this art school show that would turn out to be one of the legendary milestones in the life of the band. Representatives from scores of record labels jostled their way into the main hall of the art school's SRC. Reassured by what they heard, the offers started flooding in. The band were offered almost anything they wanted, as long as they signed on the dotted line. Luckily, Franz were equipped with the Glasgow's healthy cynicism of the music industry, which enabled them to walk away from the immediate, lavish offers and consider which way they should go.

Alex, V Festival, 21 August 2005

Paul, complete with Hagström guitar, at the V Festival

Robert, V Festival, 21 August 2005

ABOVE: Nick at the V Festival,
August 2005

RIGHT: Gavrilo Princip, the man who
shot Archduke Franz Ferdinand in 1914,
adorning a stage backdrop

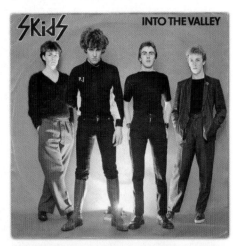

BELOW: Jock Rock heritage: assorted vinyl cover art from the Fire Engines, Jesus & Mary Chain, the Revillos (formerly the Rezillos) and the Skids

Paul and Alex, the Reading Festival, August 2004

24.
GLASGOW VOICES: COLIN HARDIE

Mogwai's first manager, Colin Hardie's voice appears on 'Tracy' on their first album, *Mogwai Young Team*, dealing with a band punch-up. Today, Colin runs the highly successful Glasgow web company simbiotic with Natasha Noramly (Fuck-Off Machete). The company offers an Internet sales and publicity platform for bands, arts organisations and festivals. It also hosts the notorious Jock Rock message board site. Colin also has his own label, Lost Dog Recordings.

The idea of simbiotic seems to go well with the type of music scene that Glasgow has, where there's very diverse grassroots activity.
I think in Glasgow, in general, people tend to help each other out. I managed Mogwai for seven or eight years so I've seen that happen at all levels. Where I've been able to help people out and people have helped me out, you know if you need a tour manager or someone to drive a van, there's always lots of good people and people you could trust and could bring in to do jobs for you. At simbiotic we do get quite a lot of people recommending us to others. It's kind of convenient in a way, because people can't be bothered working out how to set up their own online shop, it takes a bit of time and application to send out t-shirts, and we do all that stuff. One of our clients, he used to do his online shop for a while, but ended saying that he realised he was a musician not a shopkeeper, as much as he quite liked putting in notes with the orders for that personal touch, he was spending so much time doing it when he should have been writing songs or going on ProTools and setting out some music.

Is the Internet particularly suited to the sort of scene that Glasgow is?
It's not Glasgow specific. I think music of a non-mainstream variety benefits from the Internet in general, and that's not a Glasgow thing, that is just a general statement. It's a great place for finding out about new bands and it's a great place for downloading music and getting the

clips and reading about bands. There are so many bands that – I mean I've got a small record label as well and even getting a review in the *NME* is fucking hard. There's lots of bands that don't even get in the *NME* these days, you can argue whether the *NME* actually matters, because it's become a very marketing-led vehicle that doesn't really carry much gravitas with it anymore. Whereas I'd say with the Internet, it's pretty much a free land for anyone who's well organised with a website to be able to put up clips of their band, have some information about their band, get other people to link to it and have something that you can direct people to. If you go to *NME*.com and type in a band name, chances are there'll be no information on that website other than lots of blank spaces – pictures for this band – zero, interviews with this band – zero. The rest of the Internet's great for that.

How's the label going?
The label's going OK. I started it when I was managing Mogwai and my first release was an EP of cover versions, because I had Stuart from Mogwai, Aidan from Arab Strap and 'Sheepy', and they did three cover versions. Basically, it got me my distribution deal with Vital Distribution. I generally average about one or two records a year, I've got a few international distribution deals with people. It's more er – I hate saying it's a hobby – but it is something I do for enjoyment and enjoy doing, and you know keep the website updated.

Is it something where you initiate projects or do you wait for people to come to you saying they need a label?
No, that would leave it far too open for losing even more money. I'd only want to put out stuff that I liked, that I felt deserved to be heard. It's quite expensive to pay for the recording of records a lot of the time, so I'm kind of looking at oversees, trying to find stuff that I really like that I could put through the distribution here. Because, getting distribution in the UK is really, really difficult, and even with the distribution company I use you tend to oversell records into places that you'll never sell records from. People come back and say we've got two hundred copies sold into Virgin and HMV and for the artists that I'm putting out, no one will shop there for that particular record. But it's better having a distribution deal than not having one, so you take the rough with the smooth.

Is the Jock Rock site connected with simbiotic?
We host it. We run their online shop. I think a lot of A&R guys use it as a source of what's going on. It's a bit of a talking shop where people bitch on. I suppose every community in the country has one, you know Aberdeen has one, Liverpool. Musicians are notoriously bad at bitching about other people's success, because everybody quite rightly who's in a band believes that what they're doing is the best thing, and very few bands are better than them because you've got to have that sort of attitude in some ways. I don't agree with that attitude and I do know bands that don't, but you'll generally find that bands that have that attitude tend to populate these boards. It's a good source of information – it's a very popular board. Jock Rock as a whole is the nearest thing that there is to a portal of indie music in Scotland.

*Have you noticed a shift against bands like Franz Ferdinand and
Mogwai when they become successful – the bands they were playing with
turning on them?*
There's always minorities. The whole thing about people turning against bands and starting to say 'they're not as good as they were, blah, blah, blah', that's kind of expecting every band to stay the same. Actually, I've also been involved in the creative process, I played in a band years ago, I'd done my touring and quite a lot of different experiences, bands always want to push themselves rather than stay the same... Teenage Fanclub started off as quite a scuzzy kind of rock band, quite Beatles-y, and their new album is really, really different. If you do music fulltime as your job, you get bored really easily playing the same stuff, and I think you're allowed to experiment. I think if you had to do the same thing every day, you might as well do a normal job. It's a band's right to do what they feel like. Mogwai are on their fifth album coming up, I think Franz Ferdinand might have it a bit tougher, because it's like Oasis have never had as big an album as *Definitely Maybe*, but all their albums are still really big. It's really hard to better a big debut album when it sold millions and millions of copies, because you never really get the same amount of momentum behind it – it was really, really organic with Franz Ferdinand. I mean, I've not heard Franz's album – I've heard the singles obviously – but I've not listened to the album. I know Alex really well, he's a lovely guy. He used to put on gigs for

131

Mogwai years ago, so Alex has been around for ages, I don't know the rest of the band, but it's kind of a lot of faces that have been around a while. As I said to someone a few weeks ago, I do like seeing nice people do well. I know Belle and Sebastian and they're all really nice people, and I'm really, really pleased to see nice people who have talent actually making a living and having a bit of fun.

You've been in the Glasgow scene for a while – have there been major changes, or is it more cyclical?
It's kind of cyclical, but it's like the peaks get smaller with each cycle, and then Franz Ferdinand have been a big peak, but I've not had a sense that first Franz get signed and then someone comes up and snaps up loads of bands. The industry's got far too tough and far too hard to make money in for that to happen. There isn't as much money about in the music industry and there's money bleeding out all over the place through illegal downloads and piracy. I think compared to the early 1990s, there's not – even the late 1980s with all those bands like Love And Money, Hipsway, Deacon Blue – there's not as much money to throw about now. Beggar's Banquet might sign a band and that band would be lucky to get enough money to get wages out of it, it's very much a development deal. It might sign more bands, but the overall total amount of what the deals are worth is considerably less, it would certainly not be enough to actually make it practical for a band to be fulltime, or if they are they've got a quality of life pretty similar to being on the dole. But they're doing something they love, you know.

Do bands have to move out of Scotland to be successful?
It's not so much that they have to move out. A lot of bands actually lack ambition, and there's a proportion of bands – and it's not a majority – but there is a proportion of bands who are quite happy playing as many gigs in Glasgow as possible, getting their pals along, packing out a small venue, and feeling quite good about it, 'yeah, great, great'. I mean, I started managing Mogwai in 1995, they didn't really do that many Glasgow gigs, and by the middle of 1996 they'd still not done that many Glasgow gigs, because there's a real benefit – in Mogwai's case where it's not an obvious pop band – to just not play that much.

You mean more studio focussed?

Just rehearsing and getting good. The classic pitfall for many bands is that they get bored playing the songs they've got and they want to play new songs live. So what they do is they just rush songs out the door before they're actually ready, and then they perform the songs live. Sometimes if they'd had bit more time and hadn't been so impatient, the songs would be so much better, and the set would be better. It's just a common fault because people are really enthusiastic and they get out and play live and that's what it's all about – but with Mogwai, it was just a really slow approach, steadily improving all the time, and after a while we'd done more gigs in Bergen than we had in Glasgow, and it was just because we were doing shows in London, it was just a natural decision really – there's no point being really well known in Glasgow and that's it. Having a really busy gig when all you're pals come along, it's kind of not really what it was about. There are a lot of bands in Glasgow that might think that they aspire to *Top of the Pops*, but they don't really think about how to get there. I think the naivety level is reducing, but they do think it's just a case of someone coming along and seeing them, signing them and then all they have to do is get some records out, get on Steve Lamacq. It's such a more complicated process, there's so much luck involved, doing a gig in the right place at the right time in some cases. Every time Mogwai went down to London in the early years, there'd be like an *NME* and a *Melody Maker* journalist at the gig having a pint, didn't even know Mogwai were playing, hadn't even heard of them: they'd seen the gig, really enjoyed it and they'd gone away and convinced their editor to write something on it. That happened the first four or five times we went down to London where something just happened, and we always came back with either a review that was going to happen or a session that we'd been asked to do, a lot of that was luck, but Mogwai were and are a really good band.

Glasgow is not awash with NME journalists looking for the next Franz Ferdinand?

No. I don't go out nearly as much as I used to, so I wouldn't know. I remember taking journalists round, being a little Glasgow guide and doing a thing for the *NME* where I took some journalists round and we went to three or four different clubs. I suppose about six years ago, seven years ago there was a lot more focus on it, Mogwai were on Chemikal Underground and people would come up and do stuff. I think there are loads and loads of bands – I used to work in a guitar shop, and they show year on year increases in the number of guitars getting sold, and there's still a lot of kids – thirteen and fourteen years old – coming in and buying guitars. A lot of nu-metal kids as well. You talk about Franz Ferdinand kicking stuff off and getting a new interest in guitar music, there's a whole scene that doesn't get covered in the *NME* that is just as big. I mean *Kerrang*'s circulation is biting on the heels of *NME* all the time. There's a huge fanbase for that sort of music in Glasgow especially. If you go to the Gallery of Modern Art on a Sunday afternoon, it's like what punks used to do in the 1970s: just go and hang about in a public place all day looking weird, and it's happening now again, it's just nu-metal kids.

Do you think some indie bands have a fear of commercial success? Or is that just an excuse for not doing well?
You're making commercial decisions as soon as you record music and try to get someone to release it. You could give it away for nothing if you really wanted to. There's nothing wrong with earning money for creating music, if it lets someone create more and someone's good at it. I've been there where I've had to do loads of jobs and try to fit in my work and do all this kind of stuff. Mogwai were always really very good at lying to bosses, phoning in sick and focusing on doing band stuff when they had to in the early days. There's nothing wrong with making money. If you ask anybody, how would you rather make money, working in a call centre or being creative enough that someone's paying for you to go into a studio and create some music, someone funding a tour round places you'd never have a chance to visit out of your own pocket.

There's a strong link between art and music in Glasgow. Do you think that's a defining part of the Glasgow scene's character?
I'm sure it exists in other towns. Your book might be about Glasgow and Franz Ferdinand in that scene, but I'm sure it's not that – there's nothing special in the water here, you know. I think any city, especially any city where there's maybe been some industrialisation in the past, you'll find a creative community.

25.
RIP IT UP...

In the summer of 1977, Glasgow's music scene was reborn. The message of punk had reached the Clyde – even if the music itself had found it harder to breach the city defences. It was not only the rebellious image of punk that inspired a new generation, it was also the more revolutionary message underlying punk that had an impact: the do-it-yourself creed. Like a lot of the conceptual art that was finding a foothold in Glasgow thanks to the Third Eye Centre, it provoked the reaction from dismissive onlookers of 'That's rubbish – I could do that!'. Tuned-in young people in Glasgow, like those all around the British Isles, heard punk and thought 'That's great – I could do that!' – and they did.

The conditions were right in Glasgow for punk – and the DIY ethic that went with it – to take hold and flourish. Politically, the 1970s saw rapid switching between Labour and Conservative governments, as the electorate seemed to lose faith in both. However, the crises that accompanied Harold Wilson and Jim Callaghan's Labour administrations (1974–1979) persuaded much of the UK to turn towards the Conservatives. This was markedly not the case in Scotland, where support for the Conservatives continued to dwindle and the Scottish National Party was getting ever more popular. The Conservatives were seen as the enemy of Glasgow's ailing shipbuilding industry. In 1971, a new Conservative administration had threatened thousands of Clydeside jobs by refusing to subsidise the industry to the extent that the previous Labour government had done. Industrial action and protests led by the charismatic local union rep Jimmy Reid eventually caused Ted Heath's government to stage a dramatic U-turn. While the rest of the British Isles gradually turned a deep shade of blue, Glasgow (together with much of the rest of Scotland) burned a livid red. With or without a Conservative government, however, the shipyards were dying. The effect on younger generations of this Con-Lab ping-pong match was to create a growing sense of edgy apathy. In Glasgow the sense of youth exclusion was heightened by the continuing conservatism (with a small 'c') of the City Council, which was still headed by a Lord Provost as it had been since the eighteenth century. Towards the end of 1976,[40] Glasgow's youth held their breath as the Sex Pistols had been booked to play the Apollo in December. Following the bands' infamous appearance on *The Bill Grundy Show*, however, the Lord Provost announced that the band was not welcome in Glasgow, and duly cancelled the show. In hindsight, it could be argued that the Sex Pistols caused more of an impact on the Glasgow music scene by not appearing than they would have done had the show gone ahead.[41]

The Council's displeasure became an unofficial ban of punk music in general, using its powers of alcohol licensing to enforce its will. To heighten the feeling of struggle against the odds that the Glasgow punks must have felt, the disco era was still reigning supreme in the city's clubs. There's nothing like a feeling of oppression to get a good movement going, and the punk scene of Glasgow thrived on its underground status. Excluded from the city's main venues, punk bands played wherever they could – in tiny pub or bar spaces with no actual stage, or in municipal halls, sometimes describing themselves as youth clubs to avoid the censorious attention of the Council. Many of the larger punk shows took place in the Bungalow Bar, a venue in the outlying town of Paisley, as a result of which Paisley became the capital of Glasgow's displaced punk scene.

One of the first local punk bands to become successful on a wider stage was the Jolt. Although seen as a punk band at the time and certainly part of the punk scene, the Jolt were actually closer to Mod-revival bands such as the Jam. They had their roots firmly planted in the Northern Soul tradition of Glasgow and played mostly 1960s R&B covers, as well as some of their own compositions. The band frequently toured with the Jam, and enjoyed a close relationship with the senior band – the Jolt even signed to their home label, Polydor. They moved out of Glasgow to hit the big time in London, only to find themselves over-

---

40. 1976 had also seen the success of mainstream Glasgow pop band, Slik, with their single 'Forever and Ever'. The band's singer/guitarist James 'Midge' Ure went on to join London-based bands Rich Kids, Visage and Ultravox.

41. The Council impressively held its grudge with the Sex Pistols for two decades – it considered preventing the reformed Pistols' tour of 1996 from playing in Glasgow.

shadowed by the bigger act – a story scarily similar to the fate of many 1960s Glasgow bands.

After the Jolt, it was the turn of Johnny and the Self Abusers to take up the gauntlet. The band's sublime name was the brainchild of Alan Cairnduff, who then brought together the characters who would make the name real. Unfortunately, in doing so he put himself out of a job and promptly exited stage left. The group he had assembled was an explosive mixture from the start. It contained one faction who had all been to school together and even played in a band together before. Head of this faction was singer/songwriter Jim Kerr, with Charlie Burchill (guitar), Brian McGee (drums) and Tony Donald (bass). To this seemingly closed unit was brought rival singer/songwriter John Milarky. Ignoring the potential cracks, Johnny and the Self Abusers played an historic debut gig in February 1977 at the Doune Castle pub in Glasgow. Milarky had booked the gig for the band before it actually existed, but such was the hunger for new bands in the Glasgow scene by this time that the aura of mystery and hype surrounding the Self Abusers was enough to ensure a sell-out show. The band played a repertoire of Ramones, Kinks, Sex Pistols and Brian Eno covers, as well as a couple of their own compositions. Their trademark song, and a pointer to where their true musical love lay, was the Velvet Underground's 'White Light/White Heat'. The New York connection would grow ever more important to the next generation of Glasgow bands, as they started to turn away from the increasingly self-satirising UK punk scene and instead looked to the New York scene centring on the CBGB's venue. It was here that the Ramones had kicked the whole thing off, but where bands like Television and Talking Heads were moving into post-punk territory with more art-influenced pop. Johnny and the Self Abusers were soon at the top of the local band heap, and were at the heart of the crucial, formative Glasgow summer of 1977.

Summertime officially began that year on 7 May. That was the night the White Riot tour came to town. Actually, it came to town in Edinburgh, but it was still a must-see event for the Glasgow punk scene. With Glasgow still under the grip of disco fever, it was a small band of intrepid music pilgrims who set out on the journey to the capital. It might have been a small group, but pretty much anyone who would be anyone in Glasgow and Edinburgh music was at the Edinburgh

Playhouse Theatre that night. For many of them, it was not headliners the Clash who were to prove the most influential, but rather the supporting acts, who were already moving away from the punk mainstream and were pioneering the sounds that would become post-punk. The Buzzcocks had a vital sense of camp irony about them, and Vic Goddard and the Subway Sect had developed a jangly, fey Velvet-esque pop that would resurface again and again in the following decade – from Orange Juice to the Smiths. All of which was already a long way from the rasping, anti-intellectual roar of the Sex Pistols of the year before.

Punk in Glasgow had proved to be a means of rebelling against the established heavy metal scene that had become the only alternative to disco in Glasgow. This rebellion had its greatest victory when the Clash returned to Scotland in October to play the Apollo, the venue most associated with heavy metal. The Apollo (formerly Green's, one of Glasgow's many ballrooms) was also famous for its tough audience, who would show their appreciation and displeasure with equal volleys of bottles and spit.

In addition to Johnny and the Self Abusers, the other stars of the Glasgow scene during that summer were the Skids. Formed in Dunfermline but frequent visitors to Glasgow, the Skids would go on to attract John Peel's influential patronage and enjoy a Top Ten hit in February 1979 with the anthemic 'Into the Valley'. The sparky but creative partnership of singer Richard Jobson and guitarist Stuart Adamson would produce a powerful, raw prototype of the stadium rock that would define bands such as Simple Minds and U2. One of the venues that the Skids played in Glasgow was a disco positioned on the upper floor of the Apollo building. First called Clouds before being renamed Satellite City, the venue's clientele was a curious mixture of punks and disco freaks. The resulting chemistry proved a comfortable home and influence for the next generation of Glasgow bands, moving away from the sterile roar of punk, but unwilling to let go of its energy and drive.

One of the bands who were regulars at Satellite City was the Nu-Sonics. Fronted by the already inexpressibly hip Edwyn Collins, the Nu-Sonics had ridden the crest of the punk wave through the summer of 1977, appearing with bands such as Johnny and the Self Abusers and Rev Volting and the Backstabbers. It was this trio of survivors (the Self

Abusers were undergoing their transformation into Simple Minds around this time) that was selected to support reggae outfit Steel Pulse at Satellite City in January 1978. After some of the hostile venues that the Nu-Sonics had played over the previous year of their existence, Satellite City was positively tame. Just a month earlier, a Christmas show at the Maryhill Borough Hall supporting the Backstabbers had turned into a rampage when the notorious Maryhill Fleet gang – resplendent in teddy boy outfits and outraged that there was no 'sha-woddy-woddy' on offer – had invaded the stage and chased the bands into their dressing rooms.

The Nu-Sonics had formed as a punk band, but quickly grew into something else. Collins was one of those at the White Riot show influenced by the Buzzcocks and Subway Sect: to him they represented the revolution against the revolution. From Subway Sect, the Nu-Sonics adopted the very non-punk, loose guitar sound (soon to be balanced by the influence of the clipped sound of Chic guitarist Nile Rodgers), while from Vic Goddard himself Collins found further inspiration for his fey but sharply ironic lyric and vocal style. In fact, from their very conception, the Nu-Sonics had espoused the New York school of punk over the UK version – the advert placed in a Glasgow music rag for new members read 'A New York band forming in the Bearsden area'. [42] The band was never in any danger of becoming a set of Second Wave punk clones.

In the audience that night at Satellite City was Alan Horne. His own band, Oscar Wild, which combined punk elements with Horne's passion for Bowie, had failed to rise to the top like Johnny and the Self Abusers and the Nu-Sonics. Instead, Horne's talent was for the organisation side of the music business – he had already launched his own fanzine, Swankers. Impressed by what he heard at Satellite City (particularly covers of an obscure Velvets' track 'We're Gonna Have A Real Good Time Together' and Chic's funk disco classic 'Dance, Dance, Dance (Yowsah, Yowsah, Yowsah)'), Horne introduced himself to Collins when they bumped into each other at a Bowie concert a couple of weeks later.

Together, the Nu-Sonics, soon to rechristen themselves Orange Juice, and Alan Horne would put Glasgow firmly on the musical map.

42. Simon Reynolds, *Rip It Up And Start Again*, p. 344.

26.
DOMINO EFFECT

As the barrage of offers continued, one company in particular impressed Franz Ferdinand. Domino Recording Co. had not been around that long – it was approaching its tenth anniversary at the time – but had established itself as an independent label of impeccable taste. Domino was founded in October 1993 by ex-Fire Records exec Laurence Bell and partner Jacqui Rice. The label started putting out solid American underground artists, in line with Bell's own taste and disappointment with what was going on in the UK at the time. In turn, the UK record-buying public largely ignored Domino through its early years as the clamour of Brit Pop reached fever pitch, but the label built up a steady reputation for its unflinching search for good – rather than commercial – music.

Another factor influencing Domino's diet of American imports was money: Bell had taken out a loan to start the company and licensing US artists for UK release was cheaper than recording UK artists and launching them from scratch. However, Bell's reputation spread not just among the indie community, but also among musicians. Bill Oldham (aka Bonnie Prince Billy), on hearing good things about Domino, approached Bell and asked to join the roster. Oldham has since gone on to become one of the label's most respected artists. Eventually funds were sufficient and conditions were right for Bell to look for UK acts to sign. One of the first to join were the Pastels, whose Stephen McRobbie (often known simply as Stephen Pastel) Bell had known from his Fire Records days. The Glasgow-based Pastels were the very epitome of a successful independent band, who had a loyal following and did not chase any 'hit' formula. As well as acting as an indie figurehead for Domino, Stephen Pastel also established the Domino subsidiary Geographic, which focused on bands Stephen knew and/or liked. The roster includes Bills Wells and Eugene Kelly (of the Vaselines), as well as pioneering world musicians and other indie UK acts.

Thanks to the Pastels, Domino had a particularly high profile in Glasgow (local band Ganger had been on the roster) and so Franz knew exactly who Bell was before he introduced himself to them. They were immediately impressed. Not only had Bell made the effort to turn up himself (he remains Domino's A&R man as well as managing director), he also assured the band that Domino would allow them to be themselves and create the music they wanted to create. Such a promise coming from a major would rightly have sounded alarm bells, as they are commercially bound to do exactly the opposite, but Bell's track record spoke for itself, and there were plenty of people in Glasgow who could vouch for Domino. Initially, Franz were not sure that their sound was something that Bell would touch – after all, it was just pop music. At the time, however, Bell was interested in moving Domino in a Motown-like direction, with a more accessible sound and the chance of a few hit records. He recognised that Franz Ferdinand were the perfect vehicle with which to achieve this shift in focus, being a genuine DIY band who could write catchy tunes and then perform them with passion.

It was a brief courtship, and Franz signed to Domino just over two months after the School of Art gig. By this time, the band had already found themselves a manager, the London-based Cerne Canning, whom Franz would soon christen 'the Big Man himself'. Canning is a veteran of the UK music scene, most notably managing Wolverhampton's C86 band the Mighty Lemon Drops. His experiences with the Drops, especially as they enjoyed both UK and US success, stood him in good stead to guide Franz through similar challenges.

Meanwhile, Franz Ferdinand's status was rapidly rising. Many of Glasgow's smaller venues were beginning to prove too small to accommodate the large crowds that the band was attracting. A show at Stereo in May had to be performed under the Black Hands pseudonym, and the band started supporting established UK acts: the Futureheads in Camden and the Libertines at the Barrowland Ballroom. The latter was a key event for Franz, as the Barrowland was Glasgow's favourite large venue, with a long and esteemed history. Their pairing with the Libertines was no chance affair, as already the two bands were being praised for bringing a new punk-style DIY ethic back to music, much needed in the face of the Simon Fuller factor. However, there were enough differences between the bands' approaches to ensure that they never became a defined movement.

Following the deal with Domino, arrangements for the recording of the band's first album were proceeding fast. Apart from the Barrowland show, Franz Ferdinand spent most of June in Mälmo, Sweden recording.

27.
GLASGOW VOICES:
SORCHA DALLAS

A Glasgow curator and gallery owner, Sorcha Dallas started the innovative Switchspace series of exhibitions with Marianne Greated that helped to launch the Château. She shows a range of Glaswegian and foreign artists both at her gallery and outdoor installations around the city.

A lot of the art/music scene in Glasgow seems to inhabit a space that represents an economic gap, buildings that were one thing and haven't yet become something else.

It's the same old story, artists or musicians go into an area that generally the city or the council aren't looking to renovate or do anything with, and do it up to a certain degree, make it desirable. I guess it's happening with Hoxton in London, that whole area was really underground and now it's up and coming, it's kind of yuppified in a way and artists and musicians are already looking further east and other places to move to. That is happening here, which I think is something that everyone is quite concerned about, because this whole area [Saltmarket] is probably the most historic part of Glasgow. It's not been such a rapid thing as maybe happens in other cities, more of a gradual filtering through, but this has been the main arts and music scene. What's happening now is the City are trying to gentrify it all. There are million-pound property developments happening all around this area. I'm sure in a few years time it's going to be a shadow of what it is today.

There still seem to be a lot of empty buildings waiting to be used.

The only real difficulty is trying to get into those spaces. I guess you can use guerrilla tactics to literally go in and squat in them. The Château had a private landlord who they came to an agreement with. More recently, with the gallery I've been running here, I have still been doing offsite projects, which is a bit in the spirit of Switchspace. I rent this space off the City Council, they know who I am, I'm paying them on a monthly basis, so they're fine about letting me take over these spaces for a month or a couple of months. But I think it's more difficult as an individual artist or a new group of people if you're trying to do that. That's probably why so many things happen in people's flats.

You're currently showing an artist called Michael Stümpf. Did he train in Glasgow?
He's from Germany and came over on an exchange scholarship to the MFA [Master of Fine Art] in Glasgow and then decided to stay. He has decided to base himself in Glasgow. That happens quite a lot. There are quite a lot of people in visual arts who move here to study and then end up staying after that, so there are a lot people coming in and out of Glasgow, which is what I think has kept it quite interesting and dynamic – it's constantly regenerating itself.

People are also just based in the city, Lucy Mackenzie being a good example. She would probably call Glasgow her base but is over in Berlin, New York or other places, but comes back and does events. She also brings artists and musicians from outside the city. A lot of people are rooted in Glasgow, but have a very international outlook. There are people from all sorts of different backgrounds living and working here.

Why do you think Glasgow has such a powerful identity as seen by the rest of the world?
I can only talk from my experience in the art scene. Some key things have happened in Glasgow to put it on the map. Transmission has been the first part of that equation. For the first time artists, once they'd graduated from the Art School, didn't have to move to London to have a career. What they essentially did was create a support structure for artists working within the city. Transmission has a committee that rotates every two years, so it's constantly regenerating itself. What they were really aware of was positioning Glasgow internationally. What they'd do is attend biennales or art fairs or do exhibitions internationally and they'd bring key international artists into the city and exhibit them with local artists. That really brought attention to the city. I think now for different reasons, the Modern

Institute[43] has taken that to another level. Toby Webster was one of the committee members at Transmission – he left and set up the Modern Institute with Will Bradley, a writer and musician, and Charles Esche, a curator. It's a big international gallery now and the core group of artists they work with are from the city. It's really put Scottish art on the map. The whole scene is very different from somewhere like London: it's very small and nurturing – maybe more critical, you can't get away with things here. The drawback is that most artists and musicians probably don't make a living from what they do. If they do ever get that break – a gallery or a record deal – to get it early on is quite unusual, so they've generally got five to ten years of exhibitions or gigs behind them. In London, where it's such a fast market, you get people who emerge and instantly they've got a gallery; they're hot for maybe a year and then it's on to the next thing. Up here, if people do get success with their work it is really rare for it to happen early on, so they've got a real practice behind them. They've been in their studio for five to ten years making their work and they've got a real focus; they've got a fully-formed practice. If you're a year out of art school you haven't got a practice yet, it takes years to develop that and be sure in what you're doing. So I think that's what's interesting about Glasgow: it has a reputation because of the quality of work. Obviously, it's not good that artists have to find other ways to earn a living – like teaching or working in bars – but the benefit is that there's a real quality to the work that's being produced here. I think that's what people are aware of.

In the music scene, bands often have to move out to move up, but the art scene seems different.
The Modern Institute has done that, it has taken artists to another level. That's what I'm trying to do with this gallery. I think Toby was aware of that six years ago when he set the Modern Institute up. He was working at Transmission, there was a wealth of talented artists around getting exposure through Transmission, but not the kind of day-to-day support needed – sustainable support. I've been working with artists for five years through Switchspace at a grassroots level, and now there are people from that starting to come through for whom I felt there wasn't

43. The 2005 Turner Prize shortlist included two Modern Institute artists, Jim Lambie and Simon Starling.

any support. It would be so easy for them to work with a gallery in London or elsewhere, but I felt it was really important that it stays within the city, that something is built within the city. And it doesn't really benefit anyone if these artists reach a level and then have to move out. Basically, you're just training these people up so that other galleries, other places can take the cream of the crop.

One of Glasgow's most famous contemporary artists is Douglas Gordon.
Do he and people like him retain links with the city?
I think of that generation, there's a whole group of artists like Christine Borland and Ross Sinclair[44] who are still teaching in Glasgow. Douglas is obviously based in New York now, so he's a bit different. He does come back and forth quite a lot. He's connected into things and he's still very supportive in the way he talks about Glasgow. But he's not someone who's in the scene on a day-to-day basis. But I think it's important that there are people from here who are outside of the city and who support what's going on here, making people aware of somewhere like Transmission. There was a whole group of artists just after that who became quite successful and had the support of the Lisson.[45] The whole aesthetic of their work was a kind of slickness, whereas Toby Webster started working with people who had a lo-fi, kind of DIY, more grungy feel to their work. There's a lot of those artists who still work in the city, who are relatively successful, who still go out to Transmission openings and are extremely connected into what's happening.

Are you still working with the Switchspace artists?
With Switchspace I worked with maybe 60 or 70 artists. What was brilliant about that was it wasn't my curatorial vision, it was about showing artists, offering opportunities to a range of people, from those who were still studying to more established artists. It was very context-specific, very site-specific, so it was offering people an opportunity to really use that space to the best of their ability. Those were really the people we wanted to work with: who were going to rise to the challenge and use the space in an interesting way. There are two artists out of the nine that

44. One-time drummer with the Soup Dragons.
45. London's most respected contemporary art gallery.

I work with now who I met through Switchspace: Alex Frost and Craig Mulholland. Alex was one of the people at the Château. They've both got a practice behind them, Craig's twelve, thirteen years out of art school, Alex is eight out of the MFA. They were two people who I just thought were incredible and had such a body of work behind them, but they were reaching the stage where they'd exhibited as much as they could, Alex in particular had exhibited as much as he could in the city or in Scotland. So that's why I wanted to set this space up, because I felt that I really wanted to make that commitment.

So in a way your gallery is developing with its artists.
Yes, definitely. I was an artist myself, so coming from that background, when things happen here it's very rooted in the artists and the artists' needs are totally at the core of what I do. Whereas I know for a lot of galleries elsewhere it's about making money and other agendas. For me, it's a long-term investment in these nine people and their potential, in what they'll do next month and in ten years' time as well. You are kind of managing, collaborating with them in a way and supporting them. A lot of artists and musicians also have to promote themselves, apply for funding, do all these things that for a lot of people are very difficult, not everyone feels comfortable about doing that. So I guess what I'm trying to do is allow the artist to worry about their work and for me to do the rest with them. In that sense I have to have total integrity about their needs, to be aware of how they want to be positioned or contextualised and not make them do anything they're uncomfortable with.

A gallery still has to be a commercial venture to a certain extent – are there art buyers in Glasgow?
There are people buying in Glasgow, although our client base is more international: that's why it's really important to do art shows and to position yourself that way. I know it's a commercial gallery, but in Glasgow that sort of means nothing, it needs to be first and foremost a good gallery space that's got a good programme. There are still things I've done with Switchspace like the offsite element, which obviously isn't something that's going to make money. The second show that I did in May of last year was a huge offsite project with Craig Mulholland and obviously that cost me a lot of money to do, but it was really important

in terms of the body of work and where he was at. Of course, the aim is to make enough money to sustain all of us – it'll be three or four years probably before that happens. At this stage, I'm investing into that myself and into that belief that that will happen. I think that art fair side of things, that's the way to internationally get the collectors or dealers and even create opportunities for exhibiting elsewhere.

The international art scene can be very bitchy, with galleries nicking other galleries' artists, etc. Is Glasgow more cooperative than that? Obviously, it's smaller so it would be more difficult to get away with it.

It is amazing the way the international art scene works: most galleries don't have contracts with people, which I do find kind of quite surprising. In Glasgow, I think most places could get away with not having one because it is really based on trust. Obviously, the people I'm working with I have to have a really good working relationship with: they need to be able to trust me and vice versa. I think that's really important. You couldn't get away with doing that [stealing artists] here. Even a gallery coming up from London who, say, would try to pinch one of my artists: it just wouldn't happen, the artists just wouldn't do that. I would never want to work with a place that tried to do that, because for me that is sending out the wrong signals. You've not got the artists' needs at the heart of what you're doing, you're actually kind of exploiting them and treating them like a kind of commodity in a way. I think a lot of people working here do have a good attitude, they do help each other, there's a whole generational thing, people who have more experience that you can go to and ask advice from, it's really nurturing. For me, London is quite extraordinary. I mean, in Europe I don't think that attitude prevails, I guess maybe New York has more of it. For me, Europe is much more interesting and exciting, there are a lot of galleries like Lucy McKenzie's, and Daniel Buchholz in Cologne who's got a very nurturing way of working with artists and a core group of people that he's worked with for a very long time. I like that idea. Craig Mulholland is a massive fan of Factory Records and Tony Wilson and that whole attitude of it being an equal commitment on both sides. Of course I want to try to make money, I want to live out of this, I want the artists to live out of it, but, we're very much in it together. I think that's a really healthy attitude. I guess maybe you have that with labels as well: there are people who will allow artists to have really terrible albums or do really badly for a while because they know they're brilliant and they'll just invest in that. That's the sort of attitude that I like in galleries and people that work that way.

28.
...AND START AGAIN

In 1979, Alan Horne and Orange Juice were working on the first issue of a fanzine that they intended to call *Strawberry Switchblade*, the name of a song written by the band's guitarist James Kirk. The idea was to release the magazine with a flexi-disc – the 1980s version of cover-mounted CDs – accompanying each issue. The band had recorded a song ('Felicity') and had had a thousand copies printed in preparation for the launch. By the time the flexis arrived, however, the *Strawberry Switchblade* project had been abandoned and they were left with a thousand copies of a record with nowhere to go. Alan Horne decided to start a label. Its first release was not 'Felicity', but another Orange Juice song, a true milestone of pop music, 'Falling And Laughing'. Horne was motivated by a mixture of DIY punk ethic, a desire to take Orange Juice to chart success, and a sense of rivalry with the band's Steven Daly, who had already founded a short-lived label called Absolute and released a single – 'Chance Meeting' – by Edinburgh band Josef K.

With Alan Horne's parents and members of Orange Juice chipping in, Postcard Records was launched and a thousand copies of 'Falling And Laughing' were printed – full thickness rather than flexi-disc this time. The delivery of the records was just the beginning, as the band then had to shift the copies themselves, having no distribution deal set up. An expedition to London followed, during which the single was successfully sold copy by copy to record shops, and also delivered to influential music journalists and industry insiders. Alan Horne gave Postcard the tagline 'The Sound of Young Scotland', in a direct reference to Motown's 'The Sound of Young America', and while this fierce belief in himself and in Orange Juice and his disregard for convention were a crucial driving force behind the label, the same qualities could also act against the project. For example, while Geoff Travis of Rough Trade was impressed enough by 'Falling And Laughing' to consider a distribution deal with Postcard, Horne's aggressive badgering nearly put him off. The same went for John Peel, who suffered such a barrage of abuse from the young Glaswegian when Horne tried to preach the word of Orange Juice to him, that the DJ reported the incident on his show that night and only played 'Falling And Laughing' once.

Despite the hit-and-miss sales technique, however, once the pundits listened to the quality of 'Falling And Laughing', it spoke for itself. To two key music journalists in particular, Paul Morley of the *NME* and Dave McCullough of *Sounds*, the sound of Orange Juice was just what they had been waiting and praying for. The summer of 1980 was a strange and somewhat bleak moment in pop history; punk was over and even post-punk seemed to be ageing rapidly; mainstream pop was getting ever blander and more anodyne; and Ian Curtis, lead singer of Joy Division, the great new hopes of the moment, had just committed suicide. Both Morley and McCullough heard in Orange Juice, and subsequently in Josek K's early Postcard singles, a way forward. With their New York-influenced sound, ironic lyrics and cheerfully melancholic themes, the two bands managed to be pop but not poppy, punk but not brainless. Their sound was accessible but not superficial, it was simple but not without its challenges for the listener.

The Postcard label was probably the shortest-lived of all the now-legendary independent record companies, with just over a year between its first and last releases. It burnt brightly, though, and provided essential momentum and fresh ideas to a pop scene in danger of losing its way and stagnating. Although Orange Juice managed to make the leap to a major label and so survived Postcard's demise, Josef K were not so lucky: their debut album *The Only Fun In Town* was critically slated by the same pundits who had championed them just a year earlier, and the record proved to be a nail in both their and the label's coffins.

Postcard is sometimes described as an 'era'; in reality it was just a brilliant moment, but one whose echoes could be heard for many years to come. These echoes were audible not just in the future careers of the Postcard bands (Orange Juice were yet to have their greatest successes; the final Postcard band, Aztec Camera, would continue to thrive on the song-writing genius of Roddy Frame), but also in UK pop music as a whole: New Pop, as championed by Paul Morley and co, owed a considerable debt to Orange Juice and Josef K. And the great indie-pop band of the 1980s, the Smiths, would not have sounded as they did were it not for Orange Juice.

While the Postcard moment is thought of as a Glasgow affair, Josef K was an Edinburgh band and they were not voices in the wilderness: the capital also produced the two other crucial Scottish bands of the early 1980s. One of these was the Fire Engines, whose pop speed-funk classics, delivered at breakneck speed and nervy energy, attracted the attention of Alan Horne as a possible signing for Postcard. The band ended up choosing Edinburgh label Pop:Aural, newly established by local club-owner Bob Last. Although Last had intended to establish a commercial pop factory, the Fire Engines' offering, the album *Lubricate your Living Room*, was a largely instrumental energy rush of a record, both abrasive and invigorating but not an obvious chart-topper. The other Edinburgh band, and the one that would go on to be one of the most important pop bands of the 1980s, was the Associates. The raw material of the band, Billy Mackenzie's powerful voice and Ian Rankine's virtuoso guitar playing, were promising enough, but what they did with these ingredients was pure pop genius. Having started off as cabaret performers, Ian and Billy brought an innate sense of drama and theatricality to their compositions. The Associates' songs were huge, cathedral-like vaults of sound, keeping just this side of pop, but infused with the starkness of Kraftwerk and other Krautrock bands.

In Glasgow, a vibrant scene coalesced around Orange Juice. Based in the studenty west-end of the city, Orange Juice's circle of friends encompassed the universities and the art school. One local girl with an already high profile was Clare Grogan. She and a group of schoolmates had started a band as early as 1979 after being inspired by a local performance of the Derry pop-punk band the Undertones, but it was Clare's starring role in Bill Forsyth's classic lo-fi film *Gregory's Girl* [46] that first made her a local celebrity. Grogan's band, Altered Images, had sent a demo to another of their influences, Siouxsie And The Banshees. The result was a support slot on the senior band's 1980 *Kaleidoscope* tour, which in turn won them the support of their most loyal and influential supporter, John Peel. He booked the band for two Radio 1 sessions, the airing of which ultimately won them a record deal with Epic. Their

46. The film's DIY feel and charmingly inconsequential story of teenage love would prove influential to a generation of Glasgow musicians and artists.

debut album *Happy Birthday* and its catchy, disarmingly cute title track were major UK hits in 1981.

At the same time as 'Happy Birthday' was at Number 2 in the charts, another Glasgow band was making waves, this one directly linked with Orange Juice. It had all started in 1980 when Rose McDowall was chatting to her friend James Kirk about his band (Orange Juice) and the fanzine that they had just recently abandoned (*Strawberry Switchblade*). Having expressed her admiration for the name, James gave it to her to do with as she wanted. Following the punk DIY ethos of the day, Rose and her art-school friend Jill Bryson decided to start a band. The fact that they had no musical expertise whatsoever was irrelevant: they had a good name, and they had a good look. The girls were already well known in Postcard circles for their flamboyant femme-punk dress sense, especially their penchant for polka-dot fabrics, big hair and gothic eye make-up. Having learned a few chords and roped in a couple of accomplices to play drums and bass, Strawberry Switchblade precociously set about writing a set of eight accomplished pop songs and started playing gigs on the local circuit. Before they could even think about signing to a label, fate swooped in the form of Jim Kerr (Johnny And The Self-Abusers, Simple Minds) who happened to mention in a Radio 1 interview with DJ Kid Jensen that one his favourite Glasgow bands of the moment were Strawberry Switchblade. It was enough of a recommendation for the Beeb, and both John Peel and Kid Jensen booked the band for sessions – without ever hearing a demo tape. Their first single, 'Trees And Flowers', followed, featuring an impressive array of musicians, including their Glasgow friend Roddy Frame on guitar and the rhythm section of Madness, and won them a record deal with WEA.

At the same time as Postcard was flaring briefly into life, another group of Glasgow musicians had decided to head south to seek their fortune. School friends Alan McGee and Bobby Gillespie had first teamed up with Andrew Innes in 1978 to make noise and pretend to be rock stars. By 1980, Alan, Andrew and singer Jack Reilly were taking their ambitions more seriously and left Glasgow for London to try to make it with their band Newspeak. Bobby remained in Glasgow, where he worked at a printers. Although Newspeak did not survive, Alan remained in London, where he worked for British Rail and continued to further his music career. Playing with a new group called the Laughing Apple, Alan worked on an array of side projects that gradually took over his working life. He started, like Alan Horne, with a fanzine (*Communication Blur*), before establishing a club (The Communication Club) and finally a record label (Creation, named after one of his favourite bands).

In the meantime, Bobby was growing increasingly bored by his day-to-day working existence in Glasgow, and was trying find a way into music. He worked as a roadie for local bands, including Altered Images, and by the summer of 1983 had started a band of his own: his friend Jim Beattie would play guitar as Bobby wailed and hit things. Primal Scream seemed an appropriate moniker. His loyalties were soon split, however, when he stepped in to help out East Kilbride band the Jesus And Mary Chain as their drummer. Bobby had in fact already helped the Mary Chain, which consisted of Douglas Hart and brothers Jim and William Reid, to get their first single released by introducing them to Alan McGee. That first single, 'Upside Down', would become one of the most important independent records of the decade, selling around 50,000 copies and ensuring the future and fame of the Creation label. The Mary Chain's Beach Boys-esque melodies, stripped bare and submerged in a turbulent ocean of distortion and feedback, became an immediate underground sensation, winning the passionate support of the *NME* and feeding a hunger among young music lovers for a savage yet sweet pop music. Together with a reputation garnered from their shambolic, twenty-minute gigs, frequently marked by crowd trouble, the Jesus And Mary Chain's sonic assault was just the ammunition that a generation of increasingly alienated, Thatcher-trodden adolescents was crying out for. Having signed to Geoff Travis's newly established Blanco y Negro label, the Mary Chain proved the single had not been a one-off with their debut album *Psychocandy*. Meanwhile, Bobby Gillespie decided he would devote himself to Primal Scream, with whom he made some of the defining albums of the late 1980s and early 1990s, including *Primal Scream* in 1989 and *Screamadelica* in 1991.

Where Primal Scream and the Jesus And Mary Chain chose abrasive sounds to distinguish themselves from the mainstream, other Glasgow bands were following the Orange Juice route and making music that was radically simple, even childlike. The founders and guardians of this movement were the Pastels, centring around Stephen (Pastel) McRobbie. The Pastels' music, from 1982's 'Songs For Children' onwards, was a gently spoken but razor-edged assault on the excesses and pretensions of rock and pop. Deliberately lo-fi, it marked a renewed relationship with American music, this time mixing echoes of the Byrds with Velvet Underground-like melodies and vocal delivery. The lo-fi approach is now one of the identifiable characteristics of much Scottish music and art, being used as a means of grasping an honesty and direct-ness that often gets lost in more 'sophisticated' delivery.

As well as the Pastels, Stephen McRobbie was behind the 53RD & 3RD label, through which he provided an infrastructure for a series of Pastel-toned Glasgow bands, including the Shop Assistants, Talulah Gosh, the Vaselines and BMX Bandits. From the mid-1980s onwards, the Glasgow scene was a veritable talent nursery, with new bands constantly sparking into existence in a bright shower of creative energy. Take the BMX Bandits, for example: the band rotated around songwriter Duglas T Stewart, but various members passed through on their way to other proj-ects: Norman Blake left to establish Teenage Fanclub in 1989; the Vaselines – Frances McKee and Eugene Kelly – joined before Eugene left to start Eugenius and other solo projects, and Frances went on to set up her own label, Left Hand Recordings, and band, Suckle; Jim McCulloch and Sushil Dade were members before leaving to join Sean Dickson's Soup Dragons, which in turn went on to spawn Superstar, Sushil's Future Pilot AKA and most recently Jim McCulloch's Green Peppers.

This period was the flowering of the Glasgow music scene, blooming with a rich variety of sounds and influences that are the direct forebears of the vibrant scene of today. The 53RD & 3RD artists showed a renewed confidence in themselves and their music in a way that was crucial to the future development of the scene. Now representing the older gener-ation of Glasgow bands, they continue to provide support – both in terms of artistic direction (even if it is occasionally seen as something to rebel against) and solid infrastructure – to the whole scene. Many of the bands mentioned above regularly serve as temporary homes for younger musicians between projects, staying perhaps for a single album or tour before returning to their principal band. To describe these inter-band manoeuvres would require a fiendishly detailed diagram of Turner Prize-winning complexity.

29.
MUSIC IN MÄLMO

Franz's manager Cerne Canning put the band in touch with Swedish producer Tore Johansson, who was represented by the same company – Stephen Budd Management (part of the Channelfly Group) – that Cerne himself worked with. Tore was best known at the time for his work with the Cardigans, with whom he had recorded and mixed no less than five albums, starting with their very first, *First Band On The Moon*, released in 1996. He had developed with the experience of working with the Cardigans, and had honed his taste for and expertise in analogue recording techniques. Tore had a natural understanding for musicians and their requirements in the studio having been one himself. In fact, he still sees recording as something he does in a break from his musical career – although it seems to be a very long break.

Tore's analogue preferences go back to his early love of Jimi Hendrix, whose music inspired him to buy his first electric guitar. Hearing the incredible sound, raw power and astonishing presence of those 1960s recordings, Tore strove to capture something of the Hendrix essence in his own music. His career as a songwriter and member of various bands was brought to a 'temporary' hiatus by his involvement in studio work. At the beginning of the 1990s, he joined forces with Swedish band the Eggstones to found and run Tambourine Studios in Mälmo, Sweden. It was here that he worked on the Cardigan sessions that would make his name and perfect his craft. He eventually sold his share in the company, but continued to use the Tambourine facilities. He took a year-long break from the recording studio in 2001, during which he set up in his UK home in Sussex and began working as a songwriter and producer. Work followed with Melanie C and Sophie Ellis-Bexter, but very soon Tore realised he was getting into a very crowded pond in which competition was fierce, and so returned to Mälmo.

In the spring of 2003, following discussions with Cerne Canning and the band, Tore received a disk of Franz Ferdinand's songs. While it was obvious that the demos had been recorded in fairly rudimentary circumstances – kitchens and rehearsal rooms – he was intrigued that such a young band should have completely mastered their repertoire before getting anywhere near a recording studio. The approach taken by the Cardigans had been very different: the band would arrive with ideas and sketches and then develop the songs in the studio. It sounded as if Franz could walk through the door, perform the songs live a couple of times, and then simply leave Tore to edit and mix them. And that was pretty much what happened.

Franz Ferdinand's first encounter with Tore took place in London for the recording of their first single, 'Darts Of Pleasure'. Bands are always nervous when meeting producers. This is especially true of a band like Franz Ferdinand, who had a very definite idea of what they should and shouldn't sound like, and were therefore concerned that a more experienced producer might try to railroad them into a completely unsuitable recording. Tales of disastrous producer/artist relations litter the annals of pop history. The 'Darts Of Pleasure' sessions would serve as a trial period for both the band and the producer to see whether they were suited to each other. In the event, Franz were delighted with Tore's approach in trying to capture the live essence of the band. It was a positive experience for both parties, and the recording of the album was set up for June.

This time, the band travelled to Mälmo rather than have Tore come over to the UK. They arrived clutching their precious instruments and equipment, including the famous Hägstroms, Bob's ex-Belle and Sebastian bass and Fender Bassman 100 amp, and Nick's battered Selmer amp. The band had a clear idea of the sort of sound they wanted to achieve, or rather, they knew exactly what they didn't want. Influenced perhaps by Glasgow's Chem19 school of recording, Franz were looking for an honest, live sound, the sound of band performance. What they didn't want was any trace of overproduction, heavy effects or digital trickery. All of which was pretty much aligned with what Tore was good at capturing.

The *Franz Ferdinand* sessions took place in Gula Studion, which had been established in 1995 as an offshoot of Tambourine in a building that had started life as a cigarette factory. Gula (which means 'yellow' in Sweden, to distinguish it from the mostly green Tambourine rooms) was then bought out in 1999 by a team of in-house technicians and session musicians. It was this new ownership that moved Gula into a bigger, brighter building (an ex-printers) in 2001. The final stage of the refurbishment were completed in October 2002, less than a year before Franz arrived to record their album.

The procedure for recording *Franz Ferdinand* was very much a Glasgow-style affair. The band were set up in Gula's live room, complete with their own instruments and even the battered amps they had brought with them. They then belted through a song a few times, with Tore capturing the sound on a 16-track two-inch MCi JH16 reel-to-reel recorder. Many recording studios today pride themselves on their digital recording equipment, but, in line with his analogue beliefs, Tore swears by the sound captured by his tape recorder. Most importantly, the taped sound gains a special quality by its 'compression', the effect of squeezing high volumes of sound onto the tape. In order to make the most of this effect, Tore had the band perform the songs with their amps turned up to performance levels, resulting in much the same noise that fans heard at their gigs.

The results of the live performances were then pored over by the band with their producer to find the best takes, which were then edited together. However, there was no need for heavy editing to polish difficult passages of music – even the tempo change in 'Take Me Out' was achieved by the band simply practising it enough times that they got it note and beat perfect. As well as the quality of the songs and the band's group performance, Tore was particularly impressed by Paul's drumming, describing him as 'one of the best indie drummers I've ever heard' and noting that 'it was easy to do those driving songs because he was driving them.' [47]

The band now returned to the UK to meet their touring commitments. They had managed to achieve satisfactory basic recordings of all the album tracks except two: 'Tell Her Tonight' and 'This Fire'. The band eventually recorded these songs back in Glasgow, and then sent the recordings over to Tore in Mälmo for mixing. Alex and Paul subsequently returned to Mälmo to go over the final mixes and finally sign off the album, which was then mastered at Abbey Road studios in London. By this point, the band had decided that certain songs ('Love And Destroy', 'Shopping For Blood', 'Van Tango') would be held back from the album as B-sides for future singles, despite being early audience favourites. The tracks recorded in Mälmo would be heard all over the world, and would take Franz Ferdinand from indie pop hopefuls to a global phenomenon.

47. Tom Doyle, 'Recording Franz Ferdinand', *Sound On Sound* magazine.

30.
GLASGOW VOICES:
KEITH McIVOR

Keith McIvor, aka JD Twitch, is one half of the famous Optimo DJs with artist-musician Jonnie Wilkes (JG Wilkes). They started the Sunday night event in 1997 at the Sub Club on Jamaica Street. Keith had recently ended his long stint at the legendary Edinburgh club Pure, which was one of the pioneers of techno in the UK and which had resided since 1990 at the Venue. By 1997, however, Twitch wanted to move on. The result was a style of DJ-ing that merged just about any genre of music as long as it was good, but still with the discipline and dance-ability of a good techno set. Every week, the Glasgow scene descends into the Sub Club for a few hours of musical enlightenment. The innovative Optimo approach has been a strong influence on the Glasgow musical outlook. As well as the regular DJ nights, Optimo also puts on live bands – Franz Ferdinand among them.

A lot of musicians come to Optimo – do you ever feel a sense of
responsibility about what you do play in terms of the influence it might have?
I've never really thought of it like that, but it's definitely one of the things we thought about when we started the club. I'd been playing clubs for years, and it really wasn't where my interest was. I was playing to audiences that I would think 'These are people that I would never normally associate with', and I kind of stopped going to clubs, I was going to see bands, which is the reason why Optimo has bands, because I was just sick of seeing DJs. So I thought 'I want to start a club which is about what I like to hear, so we'll play music by bands, we'll put on bands,' and I really hoped that that sort of audience would come. It's a lot more mixed up now, but there's still a lot of people that come from then. I don't know if I feel a sense of responsibility, but I know for a fact that there are a lot of people who have come to the club who have never been in bands before, a lot of people that come are club kids and seeing a band is actually quite a novel experience. It was good that it mixed up

these two different crowds, and all of them can end up forming relationships and go on to do stuff. Quite a lot of people have ended up inspired
to start a band from seeing someone play there or hearing the music,
and that's really interesting that I could do that. I mean, every week
without fail someone will come up and hand me a CD-R of something
that they've been working on, whether it's them on their own with a
computer or with some other people as a band.

Because they want to perform at the club?
Sometimes because they want to perform at the club, sometimes they
just want feedback, they want to know what we think, they want to see
whether we would play it at the club, or they want constructive criticism.
What we try and do – we don't always succeed – is have on average two
bands a month. So we try and make one of those one that's on tour and
we try to make one them a local band.

You've also got your OSCARR label, how did that come about?
OSCARR stands for Optimo Singles Club And Related Recordings, it
was this ridiculous idea that if you came to the club over a period of
months you'd collect vouchers. If you collected vouchers over say 12
weeks, you would be entitled to a free record that we would have made.
And then the more we thought about it we just decided that that wasn't a
very practical idea, but we kept the name. The initial idea was that we
knew the people who were making music and that there weren't that
many outlets in Glasgow. At that time you had on the one hand Chemikal
Underground, which was more indie, or you had Soma, which is like a
dance label, and there was nothing really in between. We thought there
should be an outlet for that. The first three releases we put out were from
people that had come to the club and given us their music and asked if
we'd be interested. The label hasn't been nearly as productive as we'd
intended. Because we're DJs ourselves, we promote the club and we're
away travelling so we just don't have the time to run the label. Last year
we got an agreement with a French label called Tigersushi, the idea was
that we would A&R the label, and then they would do all the office side
of it – distribution, manufacturing. Unfortunately, that didn't pan out and
in the one year we were with them we only managed to release two
records, which is about what we were releasing anyway. So we decided

that we were going to go back to running it ourselves with a friend of ours, Rachael. And again... probably in like May there'll be a series of six 7-inch singles, all of which are from local bands, and all of them I've come into contact with through them coming to the club.

Tigersushi is a French label – couldn't or wouldn't you deal with a Scottish or UK label?
It's just the way it came about, we were playing Paris quite a lot, and there's a club there that has a label run by Tigersushi and they asked us to do a mix CD, which came out through Tigersushi. Just through talking to Tigersushi about what we were doing with our label, they suggested it and it seemed like a really good thing. Yeah, ideally we would do it through a British or a Scottish label, but that was just the opportunity that arose.

I'm picking up on lack of a label in Scotland with a bit of muscle.
And there is hardly anything. I mean there's Stephen [Pastel]'s Geographic label, which kind of gets a leg-up from going through Domino. There are lots of small labels, but the only labels with any clout are probably Chemikal Underground or Soma. And that's why we really, really want to get it right this time, because we've been running the label kind of like ad hoc for so long on a really small basis. And I think if we put out records and sell a couple of hundred copies, we're not really doing anyone any favours. We want to be in a position where the label is well known... just to give the artists a bit of a leg up, because otherwise they then put out a record and disappear without trace.

Glasgow seems to be very self-sufficient because of that situation.
It is very self-sufficient, definitely. Especially in the last few months, Glasgow's kind of been invaded by A&R men all looking for the next Franz Ferdinand, and of course there isn't a next Franz Ferdinand, just like in the Manchester years there wasn't a next Happy Mondays, but it's put a lot of interest on Glasgow in the media as a happening place.

Is that a threat to that self-sufficiency?
I don't think so. People here – there's a great Scottish word 'canny' – people here, they're very sussed. I think for all the bands, if they got offered something and they had a bit of control it'd be a great thing for them.

Perhaps it will bring more resources into the city. There was a ridiculous thing a month ago when the Scottish Parliament had a debate ['Franz Ferdinand Rocks']. It was embarrassing. But for a long time music here has had very little support. If you're an artist you could get Arts Council funding, but for people in bands it's been a lot harder. The last few years it's been getting a little easier. Hopefully, through this, there'll be a trickle-down positive effect. Maybe it will be easier to get funding and help from the Scottish Executive, the Arts Council or whatever.

A lot of bands have already been funded by the Arts Council.
Yeah, for example Natasha's [Fuck-Off Machete] album would never have come out, but that again is really a recent thing. You have to kind of know the hoops to jump through to get that funding. I think if you were like four guys in a little band from like some housing scheme on the outskirts of Glasgow, you're going to find that very hard to navigate, you probably don't even know it exists, let alone the language you have to use.

You're off to Dublin tomorrow. Does Optimo travel well?
Yeah, it's really interesting, we've been doing the club for nearly eight years, the last four we've been travelling quite a lot, for the last two we've been travelling almost all the time. The first few times you could see that people didn't quite get it, now when we go usually we get a really good response. One, they know more about who we are, two, I also think that internationally the music scene has changed a little bit: whereas there used to be these rigid barriers between dance music and rock music, I think with the next generation that's come up that's changed a little bit. People have got more aware of what's happening here so it's easier for us to take something along a little bit different. But definitely in Ireland, every time we play in Ireland it's great – there's something about Celtic people, it's a cliché but it's true, they really go out to party.

The Glasgow music scene seems to manage to be independent of independent music, it has an ability not to fit into any particular indie movement.
I think it's so true and it's something that I've always loved about the music that comes from this city, because you'd get a trend like rock-pop or whatever and hundreds of bands would spring up suddenly sound-

ing like that but it's never really happened in Glasgow. You never really get bands trying to follow what is the contemporary, media-defined 'in' thing. People here just seem to have a very strong sense of independence, of ploughing another furrow; they may be influenced by each other slightly, but there's no bands that sound really the same as each other. I think historically, you can go right back to the Postcard era, even before that to the Alex Harvey Band and stuff, it was like something unique that they had.

Your partner in Optimo, Jonnie Wilkes, is an artist; lots of the people I'm talking to here either know artists or are involved with art themselves. It seems the energy from these two areas (music and art) feeds off each other.
Yeah, I think it's very true. I think one of the reasons for that is that Glasgow is quite a small city. For some reason there's always been quite a lot of creative people here, but it is very small. And all these people tend to go to the same places, like for a lot years the Art School itself – the bar and the club – that was a very popular hangout for musicians and obviously there are artists there. A place like this [Mono], a lot musicians come here to see bands and a lot of people in the art scene do as well. And there's always been a kind of cross-pollination going on between the two.

You had a club in Edinburgh for about ten years. Are there big differences between the two cities?
Huge. It was kind of strange back then, when techno first arrived and the whole rave explosion, for some reason it didn't initially take off in Glasgow, and the club we were doing was probably the first club that was doing that and it became overnight, instantly really, really popular. There's a really weird Edinburgh-Glasgow rivalry and it's kind of bounced back and forth. Now, people in Glasgow don't really think about it, whereas people in Edinburgh have this really weird perception of Glaswegians and they call Glaswegians 'soapdodgers', it's gone on for ages, but anyway, despite the fact that we're only like 45-50 miles away there's been very little travelling to and from Glasgow to see a band at the Barrowland because they wouldn't play in Edinburgh, so on the whole there was very little happening between the two cities. But when we started Pure, because there was nothing like that in Glasgow, we

would take busloads of people – two coaches – for about five years nearly every Friday to Edinburgh, which was kind of unheard of at the time.
It just seemed that at that time we caught a period in Edinburgh when
people were just really, really open-minded. But after doing it for about
five or six years it somehow changed and became really, really narrow-
minded. It was really hard for us to break out of any musical boundary,
techno became this defined thing. And since then, I think everything's
kind of been stuck somewhere, there have been good bands, but on the
whole not that much good stuff has come from Edinburgh. And now it's
gone back to lots of people from Edinburgh come to Glasgow because
there's a better nightlife. I mean Edinburgh's my hometown, I grew up
there, I moved to Glasgow to study, and just ended up loving it and
decided to stay. I hardly ever go back, I try to find out what's going on
there, but there seems very little happening really that would inspire me
to go and investigate.

*There's a lot of physical space in Glasgow, with a lot of unused old buildings
left in some cases by the economic downturn.*
Exactly, which, again, is an infrastructure you don't have in Edinburgh.
It's a very wealthy city and property prices are through the roof, especially
when the Scottish Parliament opened, a lot of house prices almost dou-
bled over the period of a year, so any space that there is, some property
developer is instantly going to be in there to convert it. It's kind of happening here, but on a slightly lower level and there are still spaces. Also,
there's always been a lot more places for bands to play. We do put some
bands on from Edinburgh at the club and they always moan that in their
hometown there really isn't anywhere for them to play, there's like one
or two places and that's it, whereas here there's a lot more places where
bands can get the opportunity to play, and hence eventually build up a
following.

Do you see yourself as part of a Glasgow musical tradition?
Not really. When I first came to Glasgow, the first people that I met were
quite a lot older than me and they were obsessed with the Alex Harvey
Band, and told me all these stories. And I kind of totally fell in love with
this mythology that I'd never lived through. And he was a huge inspiration for me. And again, the Postcard era, I was a little bit too young for

that, but again –after the fact – through hearing them fell in love with those records. But you've got to remember it was a very brief period the Postcard thing, it's kind of become this legendary label – they only released ten, eleven records and it's kind of quite amazing that even now it goes on ... but they were really, really great records. Apart from that, there's always been a kind of a coherent scene – like the Postcard thing can be seen as a scene, it was only like a couple of bands, and since then it's all been a little bit more disparate. Of the whole time I've lived here, now is the best time in Glasgow's history for bands, I think.

Have you noticed changes since you've been here. You've been working here properly since 1997...
Yeah, but I've lived here since 1986. I would go back, though, every week to do the club in Edinburgh. There were changes around then, but definitely in the last five or six years it's become really, really interesting and really creative. Why that is, I don't know, many reasons.

It seems that every pub and coffee shop is putting on live music.
Which I guess is just part of Glasgow. It's always had a rich music scene, like country and western is massive in Glasgow, there's a country and western club called the Grand Ole Opry in Glasgow. There's just always been this passion for music, maybe more so than any other Scottish city.

Does the city have musical links with other places in the world?
I think now they have, and I think historically a lot of the bands in Glasgow's past, a lot of them have been more influenced by an American sound, whereas most British bands sound inherently British, and their influences are quite often from other British scenes. And again, one of the reasons may or may not be that historically Glasgow had massive trade links with America, there were loads of Americans coming into the ports and some of the music filtered through.

Like the stories of Alex Harvey getting records from sailors.
Yes, they were like these alien artefacts and they went on to inspire him. Another interesting thing, there's a label from New York, Matador Records, who again, they're an American label, but they have a kind of

love affair with Glasgow, there's so many Glasgow bands that have ended up with them – like Arab Strap, Teenage Fanclub, Mogwai. I had a band for a couple of years, it was myself and a friend,[48] it was all done on computers and we were trying to sound like a band. We were called Mount Florida, which is a part of Glasgow. So I sent a CD out to a few labels, didn't really care if anything happened, and I happened to send one to Matador. The head guy from Matador phones me up and goes 'I love this, we want to put it out'. I was bowled over. And he said they get sent two to three hundred CD-Rs a week, they've never ever signed a band from a demo, but the reason he listened to this was because it had a Glasgow postmark on it. That was why he listened to it and why we got signed.

Optimo will be eight in November (2005), is it still gaining momentum?
We talk about this a lot. With Pure, for example, I'd say after about six years of doing that something had gone, the magic had gone, and we kept doing it for ten years, and we shouldn't have, we should have stopped it. So I've always said we will kill Optimo when it's at its peak. But I still love doing it. The moment will come when I'm not getting anything out of it, we're running through the motions and I think that's when we will stop it. And yeah I think it is still gaining momentum, because a new generation of people have come to Glasgow who are coming to the club. When we started it, we thought the audience would be an older crowd, we thought it would be for all the people who still wanted to go out but were a bit jaded with the music that went on in all the nightclubs, so we were really surprised when – a lot of older people did come – but the hardcore people that come are like 19,20,21. It's also gaining momentum because we have this CD out again, it's kind of given it another boost, but it won't go on forever, you know, we will stop it at some point and then we'll do something else.

You've done two Optimo compilation CDs. How do you decide what to put on them?
Just going through music we love. I mean the *Kill The DJ* one is ridiculous because we kind of wanted to put everything we've ever loved on a

48. Artist/musician MP Lancaster.

CD and of course we couldn't, but we ended up with about 40 or 50 tracks. Just because we couldn't decide what to put on.

As a listener to that CD, I didn't know what to expect next.
That's why it's a lot easier for this club do go on a lot longer. Pure, even though it was electronic music, which is a broad range, it is kind of finite. Within this, it's kind of like it can go anywhere so literally the next week it can be a whole different type of music from what it was the previous week. And it's great having the opportunity to try absolutely crazy records, and sometimes it will totally kill it, people will be totally like 'What the hell are you doing?'. But because they know what the club's about you know you can get them back. Sometimes those songs, if you keep on playing them, become real favourites. At the end of the CD there's a song by a band called Love, and it's not a club record, you can't dance to it, but it's a beautiful, beautiful song. The first week I played it a few knew the song, but the other people were just 'Err, what the hell are you doin?', and then the next week I played it, and you could see people getting more interested, and then the fourth or fifth week people were saying 'This is an amazing song', and people started asking for it and they would all sing the words. So you can always introduce something that should never be played in a club and if it's a beautiful piece of music I think people will eventually pick up on that.

And finally... are you a Franz fan?
I'm not a fan. I like them and I think it's great that they've had the success and I think it's great that they're still ordinary blokes after their success. I think the fact that they're a bit older probably helped. I've seen other bands from other cities become really popular and turn into the most horrendous human beings you've ever met. Franz Ferdinand are the same guys that they were five years ago. I think their music's great... but I think Josef K were better!

31.
TODAY GLASGOW,
TOMORROW THE WORLD

W ord about the new Glasgow band that was going to change the face of pop music was already filtering from the music industry to the music press before Franz Ferdinand went to Mälmo to record their album. When they returned, they found interest in them was reaching new levels. All the band had to do was feed the growing hunger among the pop pundits to hear the new sound they were delivering. The Barrowland show with the Libertines was their first major audience, but in July they played the first of their summer festivals in front of a crowd of over 55,000. T In The Park, held at Balado in the Scottish countryside, had grown from an experiment in 1994 to one of the main pillars of the UK's festival season. 2003 saw the event celebrate its tenth year, and even the weather smiled down on the assembled multitudes with blue skies and sunshine. Franz Ferdinand's fast-rising status was even taking the band by surprise; they had been bemused by the roadies offering to carry their gear at the Barrowland show, and now they were baffled by how they were to get themselves and all their equipment up into the middle of rugged, rural Scotland. It was unlikely that Easyjet flew there. Whereas most bands invited to play such a prestigious event in front of a huge venue would have had a fleet of band buses and lorries for hauling amps and other stage equipment, Franz had no such logistical support. Instead, they fell back on the Glasgow scene, asking their friends for help with transport. Soon, a small Franz convoy, crammed with instruments, equipment and people, trundled out of Glasgow and headed north-east for Balado. The band were rewarded for their efforts by their biggest crowd to date, many of whom were already devoted fans. The festival also attracts a large contingent from outside Scotland (making up about 40 per cent of the audience), so this was an excellent way for the message of Franz to be spread far and wide.

The following month, Franz set out on a tour of the UK. This was the start of full-on touring for Franz. With their album recorded, the band now knew that it was up to them to get out there and spread the word. The rest of 2003, and pretty much the whole of the following year would be spent on the road. They were supporting two bands from the other side of the Atlantic whose audiences were the sort of fans who would appreciate Franz Ferdinand's art pop: Interpol and Hot Hot Heat.

Hot Hot Heat hailed from Canada, a country which is experiencing a remarkable period of artistic and musical productivity. Since their formation in 2000, the Heat had become firm indie favourites with their synth-dance-punk sound. In many ways, they shared the Franz mission of making danceable indie music, and it was just the right platform from which to introduce the Glaswegian band to a wider audience. A show at the Liquid Rooms in Edinburgh also saw them joined in support by the Kitchen, the project of ex-Bis singer and fellow Glaswegian Amanda Mackinnon and her husband Ryan Seagrist. Playing in front of a home crowd, Franz enjoyed a reception perhaps even more ecstatic than that for the headliners.

The middle of August brought the band's second festival appearance, this time in the new band tent at the Carling Festival. Playing both the Reading and Leeds legs, Franz were amazed as hordes of fans crammed into the tent to catch a glimpse of the Glasgow boys. It was undeniable that the band were getting it right and that audiences were responding by spreading the word to the friends, family and anyone else who would listen. This was no record-label organised poster and TV advertising campaign, this was good old-fashioned word of mouth. Franz played and audiences couldn't get enough of it. The band also profited from being labelled early on as the 'hot new thing', a fact reinforced by the news that they were up for the *NME*'s Phillip Hall Radar Award – given to the brightest prospects for the following year. Advance reviews of the band's first single, 'Darts Of Pleasure', were also beginning to appear in the music press and the almost consistently hyperbolic responses were only adding to the clamour. With 'Darts' scheduled for release on 8 September, Franz could not have hoped for a better preparation.

After the Carling crush, the band returned to the Liquid Rooms in Edinburgh for their second appearance that month. This time, they were supporting New York's Interpol, acclaimed as kings of the art-pop heap at the time and, like Hot Hot Heat, a band whose audiences were Franz's sort of people. Three more appearances with Interpol followed, in Belfast, Dublin and Manchester, before Franz launched into their first headline tour to support the release of 'Darts'. Put out as an EP with five tracks, including 'Van Tango', 'Shopping For Blood', and demos of 'Tell Her Tonight' and 'Darts', Franz Ferdinand's first release was accompanied by a video showing the band in various locations within their home city of Glasgow. It was also the launch of Franz Ferdinand's distinctive typographic and design look. Heavily influenced by Alex's interest in the Constructivist art movement, as well as Dadaist collages, the design was a group effort including the artistic input of Alex, Bob and Alex's girlfriend at the time, who was a textile designer. In fact, the template for the design had come from a tie she had made for Alex. Resplendent in its striking cover, 'Darts' hit the charts at a disappointing Number 44.

The band started off their run of shows with an appearance on home turf at Optimo, Glasgow. The club night was a regular haunt for the band, and they played in front of an audience full of familiar faces. September also saw their first European gig, playing at the Roter Salon in Berlin. It was a daunting test for Franz, as this was the first time that they had played for an audience that A: did not contain a contingent of Glasgow friends and B: had not been whipped into a frenzy of expectation by the British press. However, their apprehension soon passed as it became clear that the crowd were not going to give them a cold reception. After more UK dates with bands such as the Unfolds and Ladytron, Franz returned to Glasgow for another friendly homecoming, this time at Stereo in the company of Domino stablemates Sons And Daughters.

Touring continued into October: a headline run with new art school band the Ludes in support that took them to provincial UK cities, culminating in a well-received show at Leeds' Cockpit venue. The next date was a sign that Glasgow's star was rising: Domino chose to celebrate its tenth birthday by hosting a Robb Mitchell-organised Château night held at London's subterranean Electrowerks venue, with Franz Ferdinand as the star attraction. Other bands included Bloc Party, Joy Zipper and Pink Grease, as well as Glasgow favourites I Love Lucy. Franz also stepped up to the decks to put on a DJ set, with other sets by Ladytron and Stuart Braithwaite of Mogwai. The rest of the month saw the band once again supporting Hot Hot Heat, together with another Canadian band, the

Fiery Furnaces, with whose main singer, Eleanor Friedberger, Alex was to begin a relationship.

By mid-November, Franz had returned to Europe to follow up on the work started in Berlin, this time joined by Liverpool art punks Clinic. The mini-tour included a homecoming concert for Nick, as the band played Munich's Feierwerk, a venue that Embryo had played a number of times. On their return to the UK, the band recorded their first ever TV performance, appearing on the much-respected BBC 2 music show, *Later With Jools Holland*. Though daunted by the prospect of performing 'Darts Of Pleasure' and 'Take Me Out' in front of other illustrious artists, including Annie Lennox and Courtney Pine, Alex managed to banter amiably with Jools about the band's formation in Glasgow.

Before the month was out, Franz made their American debut with a series of three shows in New York to accompany the release of 'Darts' in the States. This was the biggest adventure yet for the band, most of whom had never crossed the Atlantic before. The Big Apple was in the process of being consumed by a plague of new-new-wave bands, harking back to the late 1970s and early 1980s, and there might have been a danger that Franz would simply sink without trace into a host of similar-sounding bands. As well as the Fiery Furnaces, they played alongside two of the finest examples of the local post-punk craze, Oxford Collapse and Palomar. The Franz sound turned out to be distinct enough and their performance passionate and powerful enough to win over their first American audiences. It was a humble beginning but, with each subsequent trip to the States, Franz would find their popularity growing and spreading.

Back in the UK it was time for the tour that would mark the end of the year and in some ways the highlight of the year for the band. Going on tour with Glasgow mates Belle and Sebastian was a cosy and relaxed affair, as Franz enjoyed the warm, friendly atmosphere that often characterises Belle and Sebastian performances. Named after characters from a popular French children's story about a boy and his dog, the band had formed around Stuart Murdoch and Stuart David after the pair won a recording contract through their music course at Glasgow's Stow College. *Tigermilk*, their first album, was released through the college in a limited print run and subsequently re-released after the band had developed a considerable following. Their music was at the opposite end of the Glasgow scene to the Franz Ferdinand, being folk-influenced, largely acoustic and softly sung – their principal early influence was Nick Drake. Despite their musical differences, Alex was an early supporter of the band and booked them for the 13TH Note for some of their first performances. He also played alongside the band's trumpeter Mick Cooke in the Amphetameanies.

Thus it was a relaxed end to a frenetic year for Franz Ferdinand. To celebrate their last show with Belle and Sebastian, at Liverpool's grand Royal Court, Alex and Nick stole into the audience after they had finished their set and made their way into a box overlooking the stage. The surprised occupants of the box (expecting a stage invasion, not an audience invasion) looked on as Alex hurled a bunch of flowers onto the stage. Although appreciated by the band, the gesture did not go down too well with the venue staff, who promptly ejected the erstwhile stars of the stage from the theatre.

So, Franz saw the year out with the prospect of an incredible 2004. They had already built up a considerable following throughout the UK, in Europe and America, and they hadn't even released their album yet. That, and what was for many the song of the year, 'Take Me Out', was all to come.

32.
FLOURISH

n 1987, Maggie Thatcher was voted back into power, despite the Conservative vote continuing to fall in Scotland. The continuing feeling of political isolation that Glasgow, along with much of Scotland, felt only added to the determination of local musicians and artists to be self-sufficient. But they were not operating in a vacuum: Glasgow's academic institutions continued to provide the basis for the city's arts infrastructure. Graduates of the Art School's Environmental Art Department, such as Craig Richardson and Douglas Gordon, were starting to make waves in the wider art world and, in 1987, the School started its now-famous Master of Fine Art course, which followed a multi-disciplinary approach. These developments added to a growing sense of confidence and purpose among Glasgow's creative community. The same year also saw the announcement that Glasgow had been chosen as the 1990 European City of Culture.

How much the activity surrounding 1990 helped the grassroots artistic scene in Glasgow continues to be a favourite topic of debate over a pint of McEwans to this day, but it certainly stimulated activity – even if it was in the form of protest at the lack of funding for existing cultural projects in the city. An undeniable positive effect of the City of Culture announcement was that the rest of the UK and the UK press started to accept Glasgow as a cultural city in its own right, rather than an industrial backwater blighted by crime and unemployment. This shift of perception had already been set in motion by the actual cultural accomplishments of the city. For example, the Transmission Gallery on Trongate and then King Street, an artist-run exhibition space with a rotating committee of recent Art School graduates that had been founded in 1983, was gaining an impressive reputation in the contemporary art world. This was especially true by the late 1980s and early 1990s, when the gallery's committee focused on raising Transmission's international profile rather than following its previously fiercely independent doctrine.

The late 1980s was also a key point in the development of the music scene's infrastructure. It was in 1987 that local musician and budding promoter Craig Tannock started his invaluable and pioneering journey to establish some of the pillars of today's music scene. He started off with Tower Studios, a basic recording facility that he and his bandmate from News From Nowhere, Lachlan McQuarrie, had set up as a place for local bands to record demos. The pair were also running regular Power Beat gigs at the Buck on St Vincent's Street (which would become King Tut's Wah Wah Hut in 1990). It was to combine the recording and live performance sides of his business (and because of a rent hike at the Tower Studios building) that Tannock established the Apollo at Renfrew Court in 1992 with John Williamson, a journalist and promoter who would go on to manage Bis. Sadly, the new venue was soon damaged in a fire, and Tannock and Williamson moved to another on Glassford Street, which had been the Traders. This was to be the first of Tannock's legendary 13TH Note venues, and it was soon joined by a 13TH Note Café on nearby King Street. These two premises became regular haunts for Glasgow's young creative community, especially due to their proximity both to Transmission and the Tron Theatre. Despite thriving as going concerns, Tannock's company could not escape the debt incurred by the Apollo fire, and it floundered in 2001. Although the Glassford Street premises was sold, King Street remained to become the new 13TH Note and Tannock bounced back with no fewer than two new ventures that remain music-scene fixtures: West 13TH, soon renamed Stereo, and Mono, more or less opposite the King Street 13TH Note. Throughout the entire 13TH Note saga, Tannock's primary motivation has seemed to be a genuine desire to create spaces in which to nurture local music, and not a desire to make money. Glasgow music as a whole, including successful bands such as Franz Ferdinand, has a lot to thank him for.

The late 1980s also saw the establishment of one of Glasgow's most famous and popular clubs, Sub Club. Originally started in 1986, Sub Club moved into a Jamaica Street basement space previously occupied by Lucifer's. It was a new club for a new type of music, and was soon one of the first UK venues playing house music – which had originated in Chicago and arrived in Glasgow via Manchester's Hacienda. In 1990, DJs Harri and Slam started Atlantis at Sub Club, this time preaching the word of techno. In 1997, JD Twitch, who had been playing the techno temple Pure at The Venue in Edinburgh since 1990, arrived at Sub Club to start Optimo with JG Wilkes. They had both come to despise the grip that techno held over the club scene, and began playing a controversial, early 1980s New York-inspired mixture of music, as well as occasional live bands. Ahead of its time, Optimo is now still gaining momentum and new regulars in search of new musical horizons, and has also spawned its own record label, OSCARR.

However, despite the thriving grassroots level of the music, there was still nothing beyond it. As had been repeated again and again in the Glasgow story, bands who wanted to move beyond playing local gigs in front of audiences of friends and regulars had to move out – usually south to London. Bands were starting their own small, independent record labels through which to release their own and any likeminded outfits' music, but most of these only managed to release a handful of records before folding, and they rarely found adequate means of distri-bution. There were important exceptions to this rule. In 1994, a band called the Delgados started their own record label in Glasgow that would survive for over a decade (it's still going today) and would serve as a means of exposure for some of Scotland's most critically acclaimed bands.

The label started as a means to release their own material, and it had not been the Delgados' intention to build it up into Scotland's most respected and long-lived indie label. The idea was madness anyway: the time and effort needed to run either a full-time band or a successful label were considerable in themselves, but to attempt both at the same time was surely impossible. The Chemikal Underground label has lurched from crisis to crisis and from triumph to triumph, keeping everyone guessing as to whether its next release will be its last, but somehow remaining a pillar of the Glasgow and wider Scottish music scene. Bands such as Bis, Mogwai, Magoo, Aereogramme, Arab Strap and, of course, the Delgados, have all reached international audiences through Chemikal Underground. The label also owns and runs Glasgow's principal recording studio, Chem19, where many of the city's most famous names have recorded. This has even outlasted Ca Va Studios, the plush establishment where the likes of Deacon Blue record-ed through the 1980s and 1990s. In fact, Chemikal Underground has

now even survived the band that started it, with the recent announcement of the Delgados' split.

Throughout the 1990s, the Glasgow scene's chief characteristic has
been its love of guitar-based music. The scene's exploration of the pos-
sibilities of the guitar reached its zenith in the mid-1990s with the adop-
tion of the post-rock movement that had been sparked by Louisville
band Slit's 1991 album *Spiderland*. Bands such as Ganger and Mogwai
took rock-based musical styles and instrumentation into territory more
connected with classical and jazz traditions, fusing them with some of
the experimental approach typical of 1970s Krautrock. Being more successful in terms of sales, Mogwai in particular has brought a more
exploratory, avant-garde type of music to a wide (international) audience
of rock fans. Their largely instrumental compositions follow the
jazz/classical route of expounding a single musical theme and allowing
it to unravel and expand. The results have been epic, soaring tracks, frequently over 10 minutes long, which demonstrate musical intelligence
and a boundless curiosity for what could be achieved in terms of mood
and sound by an outwardly 'normal' rock outfit.

Today, Glasgow is the capital of an increasingly diverse and forthright
Scottish music scene. It's a scene in which cooperation and collaboration is the norm, despite what the occasional bitter word on the Jock
Rock message board might suggest. The Fence Collective, for example,
is a community of musicians (as well as artists and craftspeople) living
and working in the Fife fishing town of Anstruther. Centred on the
inspiring figure of Kenny Anderson (aka King Creosote), the collective
now has its own record label and mini-festival. The guiding principle
behind the collective is artistic freedom and collaboration, which means
that bands under the Fence umbrella cover a wide array of styles, from
folk to electronica. Snow Patrol's frontman Gary Lightbody was inspired
along similar lines when he started his side project the Reindeer
Section. Comprising members gathered from just about every current
notable Scottish band, the Section is a musical cooperative with an
unpredictable output. Many other Scottish bands (Teenage Fanclub,
Future Pilot AKA, V-Twin etc.) also thrive on taking on new members
on a regular basis.

Go to Glasgow on any night of the week, and you'll be able to sample
just about any genre of pop music, from guitar pop to post-rock to elec-

tronica and on to a host of bands for whom there is no present classification. Meanwhile, classical, jazz, country and folk all thrive as they have done for decades. Let Glasgow flourish.

33.

GLASGOW VOICES:
BRENDAN O'HARE

A stalwart of the Glasgow music scene, Brendan O'Hare, to quote a Mogwai song title, is 'still in 2 it'. He first enjoyed success as the drummer with Teenage Fanclub, a position he held for the first three of the band's albums: *A Catholic Education*, *The King* and *Bandwagonesque*. He was then asked to leave the band ('Fuck, there's only so long you can hold a grudge, because you've always got new grudges coming along, do you know what I mean?') [49], and soon after joined Telstar Ponies and subsequently Mogwai. He left the latter in 1996 to devote himself to his present band, Macrocosmica, which he now combines with his duties as the promoter at the 13TH Note venue on King Street.

What does a normal working day entail for you?
Trying to catch up with any calls that have come in overnight, checking the e-mail situation, opening the many demos that we get. The phone is pretty much on the go all day. I do have to juggle that with making sure that I'm listening to all the demos. That's something that we do do here, everything's got to be listened to.

Do you get stuff from all over Scotland or is it mostly Glasgow?
A lot of the stuff is from out of town, because local bands know here and have played here anyway. At the moment there's a lot of promoters appearing, it's like everyone's becoming a promoter at the moment. Usually it's bands that are sick of doing gigs with bands that they're not keen on, and they're getting their friends together and saying to venues we'll put on the whole night. That's quite good in some ways and quite hard in other ways, because as the promoter here, it means I've got less nights to actually do what I want to do with. I try to find a balance

49. *Dazed & Confused* magazine.

between regular slots and promoters and putting on your own stuff. You want to have as good people as possible. Back to your question, it's mostly Aberdeen, Edinburgh, Dundee and Perth bands that are sending in demos at the moment. I try to put them on with local bands. I suppose there's an equal amount of stuff from Glasgow as compared to all these other things as well, but the Glasgow stuff is a lot of stuff from bands that I know. I do the sound here as well, so I get to pick a band and then I'll get to do the sound for them as well. Then I can see how they progress from their demo. I play in a band as well [Macrocosmica], so I know what to look for.

How does Glasgow compare with Edinburgh at the moment?
A few years ago a lot of the venues disappeared in Edinburgh – the Cas Rock and Tap O' Lauriston, they were both really great venues, and then the fire along the Cowgate took out a lot of other venues, so it was really dry. But it is getting better again through in Edinburgh for gigs now, so consequently that's meaning that a lot of bands are wanting to travel, people are wanting to basically set up tours for themselves in Scotland, so that over a weekend they can play Glasgow, Dundee and Edinburgh. I think that's pretty healthy at the moment. With the advent of the media explosion and internet access, no one is limited to playing gigs in their own town now. Ten, fifteen years ago, it would be quite hard to get a gig in another town. You'd be quite unusual being a Glasgow band playing in Edinburgh or a Glasgow band playing in Aberdeen, but now it happens all the time. Most bills we have here have got at least one band from out of town. So, the Glasgow scene has kind of become the Scottish scene as well. Obviously, there's still a lot of on-message moans like the east coast's shite, the west coast's shite, up north's rubbish. Fuck off, do you know what I mean? There's a lot of really good bands coming from Aberdeen at the moment, maybe it's like Black Sabbath came out of Birmingham, d'you know what I mean? A lot of heavier, harder bands are coming out of Aberdeen, but really good. They're not even really similar styles though, which is kind of good. You'd think they would clash really, but I think ironically with it being a smaller town there's actually more room to manoeuvre. In Glasgow a lot of bands do have one way they're going about things, they'll go to a gig, see another band that's doing something a bit similar and think, oh,

we've got to change radically. There's never been so many bands about, so it is hard to find a path you can tread that's not going to be touching anyone else's stuff. I mean, quite often you see in Glasgow when bands split up, a lot of bands around about them – kind of like in the Venn Diagram of rock – they move over a wee bit, because they sort of absorb their side. So it is survival of the fittest in Glasgow, and that's extending to the whole of Scotland now really. But, it's quite healthy I think.

Is it each band for itself or more about cooperating?
There's a lot bands that just want to help each other out. There's also a real swathe of bands that are just kind of like Oasis-inspired that aren't really looking to help each other out at all. I don't mean that in a snidey way towards them, it's just sort of because there are a lot of bands doing the same thing, they don't want really want to help each other out, d'you know what I mean?

Is it an Oasis style of music or just the approach?
Kind of both, I think. It seems to pretty much go hand in hand. It's fair enough, I suppose some people want to do stuff more like the Cramps or whatever, some people want to do stuff more like Oasis, and I think that's fine. But I don't think that's an evolving thing at all. With every year you get a certain market that's covered by certain kind of bands, I suppose more hobby bands or whatever as well, that just seems to be the genre that's being covered at the moment. There's still a lot of good bands that are doing that, bands that are really proficient, they'll always get a chance of playing here as well, we've not really got any sort of snob-by attitude about it at all, I mean everything's kind of valid if the people who are doing it are into it.

Do you decide personally whether a band's good enough to put on?
I always give people a chance, even if I get a demo that doesn't sound that great, somebody phones in and is keen to get a gig, you know, and are sort of saying that they'll try and make a go of it, I'll definitely give them a shot. But I'm not scared to say I wouldn't want to give you a gig at the moment. That's kind of tough. When I first started doing this, it was easy – I was just giving everyone a gig. Because I'd just started doing it, I wanted to find out about the bands, but when I got a year or

two down the line I was having to listen to the demos and say no, not yet. And again, from the point of view of being in a band, that's quite tough to think that's someone's doing that, but I do think it's better that someone's actually sitting down and doing that rather than just chucking it in the bin. I think that's the pay-off for me, having to be the bad guy sometimes.

How long have you been doing this?
I've been promoting for about three years, I've been working here for about seven altogether, doing sound for the first four years. Just started out doing a few shifts and ended up just doing most of them. I've always liked this place, it's a good place to work, even though it changed hands halfway through that as well. It used to be up on Glassford Street and moved from there about eight years ago I think, it was there three years, four years, and then the people who owned it at the time got the Barfly, which was then the 13th Note Club as well, so it was two places we had going on. Then the changeover happened, Barfly took over the club and the current owners got this place. But their intent was to keep it the same way that it was and the policy is just the same really, it's maybe even a wee bit more open than it was before. I think that's a bit more up to the times, as we were saying, people are getting in touch all the time looking to get shows. I think before it was harder to get in touch.

Have you noticed major changes in the scene?
The main thing I've noticed is bands being their own promoter and being their own record label. People are able to press up their own CDs now and I think that's really quite healthy. Musically, I don't know. There's a lot more Screamo-Emo stuff from 20-something guys, but essentially I don't think the music as such ever really changes, the style of music done changes sometimes, but essentially it's still just a lot of kids playing stuff and through the course of playing figuring out where they want to go. There's always bands that are doing quite similar things to each other, even though they're into different things, it's like the music might end up sounding the same but beyond that they then develop into other things. People are always saying, 'Oh, it's really great at the moment, the Glasgow scene.' – I don't think it's any different than

it was ten years ago, in terms of the amount of stuff being done, the difference is a lot of venues are popping now and people are getting gigs in bars where they didn't do gigs before. There's a lot more chances and a lot more places for bands to play now than ten years ago and that's cranked things up a wee bit. In some ways, I think it's made things worse because bands think they can play four or five times in a month in different places all over the city and that's not really going to work, I don't think. You're never going to be able to get people to come along and see you that amount of times. So, for everything that's been added in a good way, there's been something taken away. I suppose that makes my point: it is just a constant balance, for everything that changes, something changes in the opposite direction.

That applies to the lack of a major record label in that it makes the scene more self-sufficient.
Yeah, I think, were a major to be added it would add a lot of good things, but it would take away things. People might be starting to expect OK things, sort of it's a major in Scotland and we've been doing the Scottish circuit and just expecting to get signed and I think that can lead to laziness. I think I would probably not want there to be a major in Scotland, but I think that's probably just me.

Ever considered starting a label?
Our guitarist has a label and tries to do interesting, more psychedelic-based stuff, some travelling bands that he knows and puts out our own records as well. A lot of people are doing that kind of thing just now, there are a lot of wee labels that are popping up here and there. If you want to move beyond to putting other people's stuff out, it's a big step to make because you've got to make sure that you're able to actually pay the person. If you're only putting out your own records it doesn't matter, it's your own money and you just get it back when you sell them, but when it's someone else's record it is really getting into a business thing and that's not really what people in bands are good at, I don't think, or, if they are good at it, they probably shouldn't be in a band. Business acumen and rock don't go hand in hand. For some people, obviously, it will work, but in the main, people end up losing their own money or not being completely up front with bands that they're working with.

Is Postcard still a legacy here?
It is. People can look back at that and go hey, but at the same time it was a bit of a mess made of it as well. That's the good thing, though, anything you see, any programme or book about a label that was vibrant for a while, even at its height when it was doing great stuff, they were all going 'We don't know what we're fuckin' doin'!' It's the same even with the Fugazi label, they're really super-sorted-out people, and they were going, 'How's this working?' Sometimes it can just work and if it's doing well then you don't have to look at why it's working. But then, after a while in business you really have to think why is this working, so we can amplify the bits that are and negate the bits that aren't. That's why record companies exist, because you need people to do that. It's like any band that gets a manager, it instantly gets a bit easier for them, because there's someone there just thinking things and taking care of them a wee bit, and you can get to do more on the music. Sometimes that can be destructive as well, if you haven't got someone who is in tune with what the band want. Sometimes when I'm doing the sound for a band and there'll be a manager on stage telling you how to do the sound and the band are going [flicks up a finger], d'you know what I mean? And it's like, why have you even got a manager? I mean, for a lot of bands it is like a headmaster to poke fun at, which keeps the childlike mentality of being in a band. It is kind of weird that you'd pay someone to do that to, what's that all about?

Musicians do seem to distrust the business side and are often waiting for signs of being exploited. Are some Glasgow bands wilfully unwilling to court commercial success?
There's definitely a lot of that in Glasgow. I think that's why the straight-edge thing has really kind of taken off and that kind of screamo hardcore thing – people really don't want to identify themselves with anything other than what they want to identify themselves with. At the same time a lot of these kids they'll go down to After Sunshine and come back and go to McDonalds. It's like you're straight-edge but you're eating in McDonalds, what's going on there? It's just always hard to define these things because it's what you perceive as being cool that you want to align yourself with. But I do think that people don't want to advertise things and don't want to be seen to be selling out. That's the

worst thing you can do in Glasgow, I think? If you've done a gig that's got some sort of corporate sponsorship or something like that, and at the same time you're playing through a Marshall amp. There are just loads of contradictions, it's all smoke and mirrors.

Franz Ferdinand seem to have walked a razor-edge between those two things.
I think they have done. I think that's the way you've got to do it. If you want to maintain your kudos and your cool you do have to be seen to be doing certain things, but essentially you're just going down the same route as any band like Travis or whatever: taking on a record deal, taking money from them, doing sponsored videos for T In The Park or Tennents and stuff like that. But if you want to get to that stage that's what you've got to do. Again, I think that's all to do with perception, if you've got people who play it that they're playing the game rather than being played by it. To me, I don't see any difference between the two. You enter into a contract with the business when you do that. I've not got a problem with it, but a lot of people in Glasgow do. A few bands from Glasgow just recently got signed, I don't know if you know the Jock Rock message board, have you seen that there? What a pit of hate that is sometimes. On there, a band called Dead Fly Bukowski got signed to Beggars Banquet, up until then they'd been posting that they were doing a gig and people were responding great, fair enough. But then they got signed and the thread just expanded with all these people saying they're shite, they're shite, they're shite, they're shite, they're shite. What's that all about? It's still kind of going on a wee bit, it's almost as if the backlash starts instantly in Glasgow. I think the bands like Teenage Fanclub, for example, they were always fairly low-key in Glasgow, people didn't really rate them that highly, because they were like local guys, but they'd still be playing London. And then you're playing big venues with the rest of Glasgow going oh, fuck them, d'you know what I mean? That happened a lot with the Franz Ferdinand thing, people who were from the scene that would definitely have liked them, as soon as they became big were just like disowning them. Personally, I don't really like their music, but I like seeing them doing stuff, I think it's great. Every time I try and discuss things I find contradictions everywhere.

The amount of venues in Glasgow is staggering. Do you think it's sustainable?
I don't know. There's a lot of places that have come up recently. On Jock Rock there's a place that's come up recently called Tom Tom, I don't even know what it is. There's a lot of pubs off Sauchiehall Street that are starting to do things. They've been DJ-ing for a while and they've thought we can do a live thing because we've space to do stuff and its cheap to do it. Everyone's going there, but then a few weeks later there's all these posts on Jock Rock saying 'Don't ever go there, it's terrible.' At the periphery of that things are very fluid, places are just trying stuff and saying 'Nah, we're not going to do it anymore.'. I think there's going to be a constant flutter of them doing that. It has taken away from the venues in general. Somewhere like here, with Barfly being down there and really pushing it, that does take from our business a bit. Not that we're badly affected, but the sort of bands that they get at a certain level are the sort of bands that we used to get. I think it is just that things are shifting a bit. Hopefully the venues that have been around for years will keep going. It's the ones that are at the edge of things that are maybe not as stable. I think we're fine here, we've got a good reputation for being a live music venue, we've not got problems getting stuff in seven nights a week, but, as I say, somebody who's doing four or five gigs a week might not be able to sustain that.

Last night Barfly had eight bands playing.
Sometimes it's like how much more can you maximise things? Just seems weird. The maximum we usually have in here is four bands, we prefer to do three bands, it makes it just a wee bit more relaxed. Those four-band gigs can be really cool, as long as everyone knows things have got to run tightly. But an eight-band gig? That is just trying to get as many people in as you can.

Do you get labels doing showcase nights?
There's a lot of low-key promoters, but they are actually promoters, not just bands, booking a night as well, they might try to do more genre nights, like nu-metally type things. Our first Friday of the month is called Joy and it's much more sort of indie stuff and Fence Records [50]

---

50. The Fence Collective's record label.

185

stuff as well, Saturday night's a night called Miso, which is electronica, a quiz night one night as well, then there's a more heavy rock gig. So the regular slots that we have throughout the month are balanced in that way.

So you don't cut any particular type of music out?
No, no. We try to get all of them in. I think the regular nights we have are more weighted towards electronica. Mainly the kind of thing that we get offered is indie rock, really, and the more metally type stuff as well. So we try to pick out things like singer-songwriters and stuff like that and ask them to come on certain nights. I think that's where my promotion thing lies. We try to do stuff that's a bit more interesting, a bit more out there, but still you want to do stuff that people in Glasgow want to hear.

Have you ever considered doing a 13TH Note tour of bands?
We've been trying to encourage that throughout the Scottish sort of thing, because I play as well, I'm going around playing these places and I know most venues, so if a band from say Newcastle is looking for a gig in Scotland I'll give them the e-mails and put them in touch with the other people. I think, if Scotland wasn't quite so small, you could do that sort of roadshow thing, but you couldn't do that in Scotland, it would have to be somewhere like Dublin that you'd go to. Unless you're a pretty big name like Optimo, promoters are going to want to put local bands on as well and that goes against the principle you're talking about, you know three 13TH Note bands playing at a venue one night, it potentially wouldn't work because there's no local incentive there. That's something I've kind of suggested to people before, and they've haven't really wanted to give it a chance. Maybe Optimo starting to do that is going to change that as well, which would be really good, if it became just one scene in the British Isles, that would be cool.

Do you get many bands from England playing here?
Yeah, yeah. I'd say that was ten per cent of the stuff we get is bands from down south who tentatively try to plan tours up in Scotland. The only English bands you used to get up here when I was doing sound seven years ago would be touring bands who had agents and probably record

labels as well, that's how the tour would get arranged, but again as the e-mail thing has taken off it's meant that people are just able to look online, find a venue in Glasgow and say that seems to get good reviews, let's e-mail them. That's pretty good because for a lot of bands from Glasgow, to be playing alongside a band from England just feels like a proper gig to them, which seems a bit strange to me in some ways. But you might not ordinarily meet people from a different neck of the woods, so playing with them is always gonna have good ramifications for keeping in touch with them and maybe getting a gig down there as well. The gig swap thing has really taken off in the last year or two, people getting a band from a different town, playing with them and then going back to their town.

Have you noticed any changes caused by the Franz Ferdinand explosion?
A lot of people wearing ties. That's the main one, skinny ties and sharp suits. That's been mostly it to be honest. Musically, there has been a bit of a 1980s shift, but that was on the cards anywhere. The sub-culture has been saying it's the 1980s again for the last three years and it's actually finally kicked in and everyone's wearing Vivienne Westwood gear again. I'm 35, so I'm sort of going oh no! I'm thinking – and this is probably an old guy thing – I'm thinking you're gonna be laughing your arse off in about three years when you see the pictures, d'you know what I mean, because it is funny as fuck. I was a total 1980s kid at the time, so in some ways I am liking seeing it again, but it is so weird that it's happened so quickly. When I was a kid in the early 1980s I was a total 1960s freak, Mr Ripped Jeans and all that sort of thing, and that must have seemed so ridiculous to people at the time. I really like that, catching yourself laughing and then thinking, well actually... I was that cock.

BIBLIOGRAPHY

Azerrad, Michael, *Our Band Could Be Your Life: Scenes from the American Indie Underground, 1981–1991* (Little, Brown, 2001)

Bangs, Lester, *Psychotic Reactions and Carburetor Dung* (Alfred A. Knopf, 1987)

Barfe, Louis, *Where Have All the Good Times Gone? The Rise and Fall of the Record Industry* (Atlantic Books, 2004)

Bennet, Tony, Simon Frith, Lawrence Grossberg, John Shepherd and Graeme Turner, *Rock and Popular Music: Politics, Policies, Institutions* (Routledge, 1993)

Cohen, Sara, *Rock Culture in Liverpool: Popular Music in the Making* (Clarendon Press, 1991)

Glasper, Ian, *Burning Britain: The History of UK Punk, 1980–1983* (Cherry Red, 2004)

Goddard, Simon, *The Smiths: Songs that Saved Your Life* (Reynolds and Hearn, 2002)

— 'Falling and Laughing' *Uncut*, April 2005

Harnsberger, Lindsey C. *Essential Dictionary of Music* (Alfred, 1966)

Hogg, Brian, *All that Ever Mattered: The History of Scottish Rock and Pop* (Guiness Publishing, 1993)

Hopkins, David, *After Modern Art: 1945–2000* (Oxford University Press, 2000)

Irving, Gordon, *The Good Auld Days: The Story of Scotland's Entertainers from Music Hall to Television* (Jupiter, 1977)

Kielty, Martin, *SAHB Story: The Tale of the Sensational Alex Harvey Band* (Neil Wilson, 2004)

Kirsch, Adam, 'Smashed: The Pulp Poetry of Charles Bukowski', *New Yorker*, 14 March 2005

Littlejohn, JH *The Scottish Music Hall: 1880–1990* (G.C. 1990)

Lowndes, Sarah, *Social Sculpture: Art, Performance and Music in Glasgow: A Social History of Independent Practice, Exhibitions and Events since 1971* (Stopstop, 2003)

Lulu, *Lulu: I Don't Want to Fight* (Time Warner, 2002)

Maver, Irene, *Glasgow* (Edinburgh University Press, 2000)

Morley, Paul, *Ask: The Chatter of Pop* (Faber and Faber, 1986)

– *Words and Music* (Bloomsbury, 2003)

Oakley, CA *The Second City: The Story of Glasgow* (Blackie, 1967)

Penman, Ian, *Vital Signs: Music, Movies and Other Manias* (Serpent's Tail, 1998)

Redemption Songs: A Choice Collection of 1000 Hymns and Choruses for Evangelistic Meetings, Solo Singers, Choirs, and the Home (First edition, Pickering and Inglis, 1940)

Reynolds, Simon, *Rip It Up and Start Again: Postpunk, 1978–1984* (Faber and Faber, 2005)

Ross, Raymond et al. 'Joseph Beuys in Scotland', *Cencrastus*, Issue 80

Street, John, *Rebel Rock: The Politics of Popular Music* (Basil Blackwell, 1986)

Whitcomb, Ian, *After The Ball* (Allen Lane, 1972)

Yates, Brendan, *Out of the Void: The Primal Scream Story* (Empire Publications, 2003)

Franz Ferdinand websites:
Official site: franzferdinand.co.uk
Fan sites: franzferdinand.org; franzferdinand.net

INDEX